CLASSICAL GREEK THEATRE

STUDIES IN THEATRE

HISTORY & CULTURE

Edited by Thomas Postlewait

CLIFFORD ASHBY

Classical Greek Theatre
NEW VIEWS OF AN OLD SUBJECT

UNIVERSITY OF IOWA PRESS Ψ IOWA CITY

University of Iowa Press, Iowa City 52242

Copyright © 1999 by the University of Iowa Press
Printed in the United States of America

Design by Richard Hendel

http://www.uiowa.edu/~uipress
Printed on acid-free paper

Library of Congress Cataloging-in-Publication Data

Ashby, Clifford.

   Classical Greek theatre: new views of an old subject / by
Clifford Ashby.

      p.   cm. — (Studies in theatre history and culture)

   Includes bibliographical references and index.

   ISBN 0-87745-641-0

   1. Theater—Greece—Production and direction—History.
2. Theaters—Greece—History.   3. Theater—Greece—History.
I. Title. II. Series.

PA3201.A79 1998

792'.0938—dc21   98-38376

99   00   01   02   03   C   5   4   3   2   1

FOR SYLVIA

Companion, navigator, critic, editor, and wife

I should not have to warn you that so much depends on stage business. Everyone knows that plays are written only to be acted, and I wish that this play would be read only by those who have the vision to see in their reading all the elements of performance.

MOLIÈRE, preface to *L'Amour médecin*

[Writing of Hannibal] On these points I can speak with some confidence as I have . . . personally inspected the country and made the passage of the Alps to learn for myself and see.

POLYBIUS, *The Histories*, 3.48.12

CONTENTS

Acknowledgments *xi*

Preface *xiii*

1 The Limits of Evidence I: The Writings *1*

2 The Limits of Evidence II: Physical Remains *15*

3 The Shape of the Orchestra: A History and Critique *24*

4 Where Was the Altar? *42*

5 The Scene House: The Dithyramb, Found Space,
   and the "Royal" Door *62*

6 Stage Machinery *81*

7 The Orientation of Greek Theatres *97*

8 Dawn Performances: Three Days in a Row? *118*

9 Ramifications of the Three-Actor Rule *128*

10 Validation by Authority: Margarete Bieber's Comparisons
   of Hellenistic and Roman Theatres *139*

11 Validation by Repetition: The Menander Reliefs *147*

12 Validation (and Discovery) by Experiment:
   Producing a Three-Actor *Ion* *165*

Bibliography *181*

Index *187*

ACKNOWLEDGMENTS

Many knowledgeable and perceptive scholars have listened to what must have seemed an almost endless barrage of speculations, arguments, theories, and, occasionally, conclusions; I am very grateful to all of them. The following were particularly helpful in providing advice, counsel, and corrections in the process of working through preliminary drafts of the various chapters: Robert A. Bridges, Oscar G. Brockett, John W. Brokaw, Jack C. Cargill, Peder Christiansen, Eric Csapo, Alan Hughes, John R. Porter, and the late Ronald E. Schulz. Their considerable help and willingness to share their expertise are gratefully acknowledged.

Thanks are also due to Texas Tech University for providing a year's leave to begin this study, to Otis W. Templer for information on solar trajectories, and to David McGaughey for the program which produced the theatrical compass bearings of chapter 7. Claude Schumacher was most helpful in guiding earlier versions of some chapters through publication in *Theatre Research International.* The American School of Classical Studies allowed me the privileges of a senior associate fellow during much of my travel, providing an agreeable home-away-from-home and an opportunity to mingle with some of the best and brightest scholars in the field.

Numerous libraries allowed me the use of their facilities and the assistance of their capable staffs: the University of Missouri, the University of Washington, the University of Texas, the British Library, Princeton University, the American School of Classical Studies, the British School at Athens, and the Institute for Advanced Studies. The Texas Tech University library provided a home base, and the interlibrary loan staff was particularly helpful in locating nearly forgotten volumes gathering dust on distant shelves; my particular thanks to librarians Carol Roberts, Amy Chang, and the late Gloria Lyerla.

Thomas Postlewait, general editor of this series, has been most helpful in shaping and tempering the manuscript; his suggestions, emendations, and corrections were both kind and to the point. Holly Carver, interim director of the University of Iowa Press, has made the stressful process of bringing this book to completion a nearly unalloyed pleasure; her patience, diligence, and expertise are gratefully acknowledged. Ronald W. Vince gave the manuscript a perceptive and helpful reading at the beginning of the publication process, and Alan Hughes performed a similarly valuable service at the end. Kathy Lewis, editor for the University of Iowa Press, provided a very thorough and knowledgeable reading of the manuscript. Babs Hester assisted on the index.

Almost from the start of my enquiry into what was for me a little-known field, three dedicated teachers, my seniors in every way, volunteered to guide my education. I am profoundly indebted to Helen Bacon, Gordon M. Kirkwood, and Homer A. Thompson for their tutelage and friendship.

PREFACE

This study began some sixteen years ago. It started with a summer tour of Italy and Greece, one undertaken not only to seek explanations for some of the puzzling contradictions found in the standard histories of Greek theatre, but also to formulate answers to questions that had been posed by my students over the years. Why, for example, was the late-fourth-century theatre of Epidauros built with a complete-circle orchestra when, according to orthodox theory, the complete circle had been abandoned as an orchestra shape more than a century before? Needless to say, a quick swing around the most touristed theatre sites did not provide much in the way of enlightenment; even now, after countless miles of travel and many years of study, I still cannot answer with any certainty the riddle of Epidauros' complete circle. Is it possible that the theatre, as part of the major shrine of Aesklepius, was used primarily for healing ceremonies? There is, to my knowledge, no evidence of plays ever having been presented there. Perhaps, as part of each day's curative ritual, hundreds of cure-seeking pilgrims descended the shorter-than-average steps to hobble around the full circle in a dance intended to restore their good health.

While this first trip did not yield much in the way of startling revelations, it did provide some understanding of just how diverse, scattered, and disconnected were the myriad archaeological and written sources relating to the study of the Greek classical theatre; obviously, any further research would involve more than explorations conducted from a carrel in the library. Soon after this first journey, a year's leave was spent as a senior associate fellow at Athens' American School of Classical Studies; this provided a base of operations, access to a specialized library, and the company of dedicated scholars willing to share their knowledge and understanding. As research progressed, I wrote a series of articles for *Theatre Research International* and *Theatre Survey*; these provided starting points for some of the chapters in the present volume.

Field research proved a necessity. There were many journeys (usually with my wife) to an assortment of archaeological sites, museums, and collections. These trips first centered on Greece, but quickly expanded to Sicily, southern Italy, Albania, and as far into modern Turkey as Hellenic civilization had penetrated; remaining to be explored are several Greek settlements on the Black Sea, a few sites in North Africa, and single theatres in Afghanistan and Romania.

I have visited well over a hundred theatre sites, many several times. These treks, usually by car, to seldom-visited sites off the beaten track often turned into minor adventures. I revel in driving back country roads; whether in the American West or in nations bordering the Mediterranean, the thrill of wandering unknown terrain is much the same. Narrow, rutted roads are devoid of warning signs or arrows pointing directions; railings seldom guard the edges of curves and precipices; but breathtaking vistas are sure to open up over the next hill, panoramas of worlds where people live out their lives among the stunning ruins of vanished civilizations.

Many Greek theatres were rediscovered in the course of the past century. Usually, they have been excavated, studied, and all but forgotten in out-of-the-way locations; blowing dirt and vegetation have already begun the work of reinterment. Some theatres, like the one at Stratos, in Greece, have been located, but await the attention of an archaeological team; at Aptera, on Crete, only the edge of one row of seats peeks out from a rocky embankment. Others have been scavenged; only vague outlines on the island of Aegina and at Sardis, in Turkey, remain to show where thousands of spectators once watched the entertainments of the day. Not all pillaging was done in antiquity; the white marble and red porphyry seating of the theatre at Samothraki was carted away between 1927 and 1937, and the cult theatre of Apollo Erethemia, on Rhodes, vanished sometime after the site was published in 1932.

Some searches were memorable. The two theatres at Balbura, in Turkey, one Greek and the other Roman, were spotted from the road with binoculars only after several fruitless trips up and down the highway. A mile's slog down a muddy trail ended at a steep hill that had to be climbed hand over hand, grasping at bushes and outcroppings. After photographing the strangely uncompleted Greek theatre, there remained the task of scrambling down over loose rocks, fording an icy stream, and examining what could be seen of the Roman theatre through its blanket of snow. At nearby Oenanda, a retired taxi driver from Istanbul led my wife and me, at sunset, ever deeper and higher into a dark forest, apparently intent that we should see and appreciate the many Lydian tombs in the vicinity. We began to wonder if some nefarious plot was afoot, but finally, just as apprehension was reaching the turn-back point, our guide ushered us into the impressive remains of the theatre. On our return, we were treated to a feast of broiled lamb heads, served by the light of a kerosene lantern. One Sicilian jaunt found us climbing, directionless, up a fog-bound hill outside the village of San Cipirello; somehow, almost magically, the fog parted briefly and the ruins of ancient Iato materialized. Photographs had to wait for a return trip in the sunshine.

Some quests ended in failure; after two trips, I have still not found the theatre at Kalasarna, on the tiny island of Kos, although I must have been within rock-throwing distance. In Epiros, a much-abused rental car refused to ascend more than halfway up the mountain where sat the impressive, deserted ruins of Veliani; its fortification walls provided a corral for a large flock of sheep, but neither their grazing nor excavation had disclosed anything resembling the standard theatre plan which some optimistic archaeologist had drawn on the site map.

Successes far outweighed failures; many unusual and potentially significant sites were studied and photographed, places such as the fourth-century processional theatre at Lato, on Crete, and the straight-rowed theatre at Trachones, near the Athens airport. The ceremonial tunnel leading from the council chamber (*bouleuterion*) into the theatre at Akrai, on Sicily, is known from the literature, but somehow a similar tunnel from Pergamum's altar of Zeus into the large theatre seems to have escaped notice (figs. 1 and 2; all photographs are by the author unless otherwise noted).

While the surviving Greek theatres show many similar features, the differences (the adaptations to local customs, conditions, and functions) lend weight to the need for a comprehensive study: cisterns built into the theatres of Orchomenos-in-Arcadia, Delos, and Santorini to catch runoff from the *theatron*; flat-land theatres of Metapontum, Dion, Eretria, Tegea, and Mantinea built on artificial hillsides. While archeological reports are certainly necessary for studying these various sites, a much deeper understanding can be gained by spending time at the primary source.

Although lacking a classical background, I have the advantages that come from a life spent working in the many crafts involved in theatre production. This practical training has given me an understanding of the processes involved in the staging of a play. Further, my study of theatre history allows me to bring to the discussion a broad understanding of how theatre has operated through the ages, an ability to extrapolate from production techniques of other times and places.

FIGURE 1. *The ceremonial entrance tunnel into the Pergamum theatre.*

FIGURE 2. *The tunnel as it enters the theatre.*

This does not mean that the theatrical practices of one era can be automatically transferred to another. Simon Goldhill sensibly objects to such overgeneralization; in a review, he takes Peter Arnott to task for his habit of drawing parallels at the drop of a hat, such as stating that Greek choruses follow the same conventions as classical ballet: "This unreflective comparative method . . . shows once more with great clarity how the use of such uncontested analogies seems inevitably to reoccur in the analyses of ancient stagecraft — a bandwagon many have jumped on in recent years — and how dangerous such an approach can be."[1]

Goldhill's caveat is well taken. Analogies can become so overextended that they are worse than useless; nevertheless, valid points of comparison do exist. No one suggests that Greek choruses stood at the *barre* doing *pliés*; but both classical ballet dancers and Greek choruses were trained in movement, both learned to move as a unit, and both *corps de ballet* and chorus find their dances enhanced by flowing, eye-catching costumes that help fill a large performance space. Anyone concerned with the appearance of a Greek chorus could do worse than study a stage filled with dancers in romantic tutus; in terms of spectacle, ballet choruses are comparable to the dancing figures in elaborately pleated himations that appear on the vases. Similarly, the basic requirements for scenery in the Greek era are almost identical to those of theatres from later ages. Then as now, scenic elements must be suited to the script and the action, attractive, portable, sturdy enough to survive the run of the play, and within the budget.

Concerns about production techniques are being increasingly broached in the continuing debates about the Greek theatre, reflecting the theatre historian's interest in the "how" aspects of performance as well as the "why" problems of playscripts and their literary merits. Care should be taken, however, to avoid overemphasis on aspects of presentation, to keep from committing the narrowing of focus that Heinrich Bulle perceives in other disciplines when he writes that "the study of theatre problems by philology, archaeology and architecture, three fields with such essentially different methodologies, brings with each of them an inevitable one-sidedness of viewpoint."[2] His statement summons up an image of the three blind men groping around various portions of the elephant's anatomy: each sightless person examines a certain portion of the whole creature, and each is adamantly prepared to defend the truth of what he perceives. The theatre historian who joins this trio must avoid becoming a fourth blind man, must aim at incorporating the perceptions of the others into a completely fleshed-out representation.

A note about the endnotes: each of the many specialties concerned with the Classical Age has developed its own shorthand methods of reference, creating a problem for anyone not attuned to the argot of that particular field. To reduce this problem and to make sources more accessible to the nonspecialized reader, all references are given in complete form, and first citations begin anew with each chapter.

NOTES

1. Simon D. Goldhill, review of *Public and Performance in Greek Theatre*, by Peter D. Arnott, *Theatre Research International* 15 (1990): 262.

2. "Die Bearbeitung des Theaterproblems von den drei so wesenverschiedenen Arbeitsgebieten der Philologie, Archäologie, Architektur ausbrachte unvermeidliche Einseitigkeiten mit sich" (Heinrich Bulle and Heinrich Wirsing, *Szenenbilder zum Griechischen Theater des 5. Jahrhunderts v. Chr.*, 21).

CLASSICAL GREEK THEATRE

1

THE LIMITS OF EVIDENCE I

The Writings

Both written and archaeological sources concerning the Greek theatre are generally well known. Ronald Vince has discussed them at some length in *Ancient and Medieval Theatre*; more recently, Eric Csapo and William J. Slater have covered much the same body of material in *The Context of Ancient Drama*. It may then seem redundant to chew over the same information in the following two chapters, but one has only to compare the readings by Vince with those of Csapo and Slater to see that each researcher places his own emphasis and interpretation on what is essentially the same body of material. Since my conclusions are based largely upon differing interpretation of the evidence, I hope that I may be forgiven for retracing the admirable work done by the above authors.

There has long been a tendency to enshrine the sketchy and often inaccurate Greek theatre testimonials that survive to the present age. Snippets of information gathered from hither and yon have been bundled together under the assumption that all "ancient" materials possessed equal degrees of reliability and authenticity. But, as Oliver Taplin writes, there is still a tendency "to regard any information written in Ancient Greek (or Latin) as above criticism."[1] Thus, the library-bound scholars who wrote *The Suda* some fourteen centuries after the premiere performances of the surviving plays have often been accorded much the same degree of credence as verifiable evidence dating from the Classic period. Fortunately, this unquestioning acceptance of words on the page or scroll has diminished as archaeological evidence assumes greater importance.

This chapter looks at the limitations of written materials available to the researcher. The virtues and shortcomings of these documents are examined, with a few warning signs posted along the pathway leading to a reconsideration of Greek theatre in the fifth century.

THE PLAYS

Many Scripts, but Only a Few Survive

By the middle of the fourth century, Athens and possibly all of Greece must have been awash with playscripts. A single festival, Athens' Great Dionysia, presented at least fifteen new scripts each year, none of which received second performances at the festival until well into the fourth century (and then only the plays of Aeschylus). Assuming that these contests were held annually for a hundred years (as they certainly were), 900 tragedies, 300 satyr plays, and more than 300 comedies would have been presented, making a total of 1,500 original scripts written in the course of one century for that single festival. Three or even four other festivals in Athens, the Anthesteria, Lenaia, Rural Dionysia, and possibly the Panathenaia, also presented plays, presumably using different scripts than those of the Dionysia.

Other city-states may have had playwrights creating still more scripts. Roughly two hundred known theatre sites have been uncovered, but while stone records (*didaskalia*) offer confirmation of theatrical performances for some, there is no firm evidence that the majority were used for play production; *theatron* means "a seeing place," but exactly what events were seen is uncertain. Nevertheless, the presentation of plays, new or old, in these "theatres" may be reckoned a firm possibility.

There would have been at least a few original scripts written to please the local populace. Such cultural centers as Syracuse needed to fill part of their dramatic diet with plays focusing on their particular hopes and aspirations, rather than staging a steady run of plays celebrating Athens' triumph over the Persians and comedies roasting Athenian politicians and generals.[2] An active production program outside Athens would have produced a further abundance of scripts: if any extended extrapolation is attempted from the one-century total of scripts presented at the City Dionysia, the figure becomes mind-dizzying.

Writing was prized, and many of these plays would have been preserved — at least for a while. One ruler of Pergamum decreed that all the writings in his kingdom be requisitioned for his personal library, and the fabled library at Alexandria contained, by James Diggle's estimate, "100,000 or so volumes."[3] But with a decline in learning, papyrus scrolls lost their value; some were used as mummy wrappings, and others may have served to start the morning cooking fires.

The Surviving Plays

A total of forty-four complete plays and some fragments have survived the perilous journey through the millennia. This represents less than 3 percent of the 1,500 scripts presumed to have been composed during one century for the City Dionysia.[4] Moreover, these surviving scripts, chosen more for literary than theatrical values, offer a distorted view of typical Athenian dramatic fare.

THE TRAGEDIES

The majority of surviving tragedies are "school" plays used in the teaching of Greek, the *lingua franca* of the Mediterranean. In terms of numbers, the school plays are a fairly balanced selection from the Hallowed Three: seven plays each by Aeschylus and Sophocles, and nine (of the seventeen surviving scripts) by Euripides. These particular plays were chosen by Byzantine scholars on the basis of their literary qualities, not their stageworthiness. Here, as elsewhere in history, the entertainment appetites of the populace and the literary/dramatic tastes of the cognoscenti differ considerably. Consider *Medea*, for example: although part of a last-place entry in the City Dionysia, the tragedy has been preserved in the school plays — while not one of the six tragedies from the winning and second-place tetralogies has survived. If a sequence of prize-winning scripts from even one year of the Dionysia had been preserved, some light would be shed upon the theatrical tastes of fifth-century audiences — assuming that the judges (we know little of their qualifications beyond being male and being Athenian citizens) usually expressed the sentiments of the audiences. Lacking a volume of *Prize-Winning Plays*, we can only wonder whether the Byzantine scholars paid any attention to the entertainment preferences of the Athenian citizenry and/or its judges when making their selections.

Of much greater value in the study of Athenian popular entertainment is a group of tragedies that were *not* chosen for literary merit. These are ten plays by Euripides which, judging from their alphabetical arrangement by title, comprised part of *The Complete Plays of Euripides*. "This is of great importance since the plays are not selected, but a fair sample of Euripides' work," according to Donald William Lucas.[5]

These plays are part of an Alexandrian papyrus edition of Euripides, the titles ranging from *epsilon* to *kappa*. Six other plays of Euripides, known only by title, are missing from this alphabetical sequence, but their absence does not indicate that a selection process excluded them. According to Bruno Snell, one play, *Thersites*, was lost before the Alexandrian edition, and the other five were copied on a single papyrus roll that has vanished.[6] *The Bacchae*, since its title begins with *beta*, is clearly not part of the *epsilon* to *kappa* grouping, but neither is it part of the school play selection. The course of preservation for this tragedy remains unclear; G. Zuntz calls it "the riddle of *The Bacchae*."[7]

While not totally indicative of typical Athenian theatre fare, the scripts from the alphabetical sequence do provide at least a valid sampling of Euripides' theatrical output, rather than a later selection of his "masterpieces." They are definitely not a collection of *Best Plays*: *Cyclops* is a satyr play, the only complete one in existence; two others, *Ion* and *Helen*, would be classified as comedies in the modern if not the ancient sense of the word.[8] *Elektra* conforms somewhat to the Aristotelian preference for an unhappy ending, but despite the guilt that Orestes experiences after killing his mother, a reasonably cheerful postscript finds the young man embarking on a clearly defined pathway to expiation, while Elektra is given a suitable husband and a promising future. *Iphigenia at Aulis* has a suitably unhappy ending only if the play is allowed to conclude with the probably spurious ending which has Iphigenia lying dead upon the altar; the more probable melodramatic conclusion has Artemis substituting a deer for the young virgin just as the sacrificial knife begins its downward course. Only one play from this group, *Hekuba*, has a single protagonist whose fortune worsens in the course of the play. Not surprisingly, this play, with a plot that Aristotle would have sanctioned, is the only one of the alphabetical listing that was also chosen for the Byzantine school selection. (Apparently, the later scholars were willing to ignore Aristotle's dictum that women and slaves were not suitable subjects for tragedy.)

The remaining five plays in this volume are literarily flawed, changing characters and plot lines between the first half of the play and the second. They are broken-backed, lacking the "spine" that unifies the better-regarded tragedies. These "shockers," to use Richmond Lattimore's designation,[9] are laden with sensational events: Herakles arranges his own funeral pyre after his devoted wife kills herself because she has inadvertently poisoned him; the many fatherless children of the *Suppliant Women* keen their sorrows as a distraught Evadne prepares to hurl herself onto her husband's funeral pyre; the Taurian Iphigenia is tearfully reunited with her brother only after first preparing to kill both him and his companion; in *Heraklei-dae*, Makaria eagerly allows her virgin blood to be spilled for no very good reason, a doddering old Iolaus is led into battle on the arm of an attendant, and Herakles' mother positively salivates over details of the forthcoming execution of her persecutor. Most sensational of all is *Hekuba*, with ghosts, virgin sacrifice, eye gouging, and an ending prediction that the former queen of Troy will "climb the masthead" of Ulysses' vessel, be "changed to a dog, a bitch with flaming eyes," and plunge to her death.[10]

These plays are among the literary discards, seldom making the assigned reading lists of literature classes. However, as a sampling of Euripides' total output, they reflect the typical theatre fare of fifth-century Athens more accurately than do the more literarily meritorious plays chosen by the Byzantines.

THE COMEDIES

Judgments about Greek comedy are based largely upon the eleven scripts and fragments of Aristophanes — plus a few scraps from other comic play-wrights. The remarkably scanty and obviously unbalanced selection of comic playwrights has not prevented the following unproven assumptions from assuming gospel dimensions: (1) Aristophanes' scripts are typical of Old Comedy; (2) Aristophanes was the best of fifth-century comic play-wrights; according to Mary R. Lefkowitz, "The idea that Aristophanes was not only a better poet, but more elegant and less crude than his predecessors and contemporaries comes from Aristophanes' own parabaseis";[11] (3) of the forty plays that Aristophanes is known to have presented on the Athenian stage, the extant eleven are (choose one or more from the following) his funniest, most typical, best reading, and/or most producible. As with the tragedies, some of these comedies are known to have failed as contest entries, in either the Dionysian or Lenaian festivals, and modern critics frequently disagree with the Athenian judges' ranking of the surviving scripts. Eugene O'Neill, Jr., felt that "the victory of *The Knights*, like the failure of *The Birds* a decade later, clearly demonstrates the whimsical instability and the dubious value of the vulgar taste."[12] The place that Aristophanes' surviving comedies occupied in the theatre of his day must, like that of the tragedies, remain a matter for speculation. All that can be said with certainty is that the preserved comedies were popular with literary scholars of later ages.

THE SATYR PLAYS

The surviving one and a half satyr plays add a very important detail to the study of Greek popular entertainment: no matter how weighty, somber, and depressing the tragedies might have been, everyone departed for home in a cheerful frame of mind, having laughed uproariously at a slapstick travesty involving misdeeds of the gods and other mythic figures.[13] The Greeks were apparently not prepared to retire to their homes burdened with feelings of pity and awe; they wanted the day to end with laughter.

Ending a serious entertainment with a bit of fluff has long been common theatre practice; in the eighteenth and nineteenth centuries a short farce or comic opera regularly followed presentation of a Shakespearean tragedy.[14] Laurence Olivier, not wishing his audiences to depart in a gloomy mood after his tragic performance of *Oedipus*, concluded the evening by appearing as Mr. Puff, in Richard Brinsley Sheridan's *The Critic*, a twin bill that became known as *Oedipuff*. Audiences, whether ancient or modern, do not enjoy departing the theatre carrying a heavy emotional burden. It should be noted also that many of the surviving tragedies have happy endings, and some were downright comedies (see the discussion of *Ion* in chapter 12). The Dionysia was, after all, a joyous holiday, not a Greek version of Lent, Yom Kippur, or Ramadan.

The Plays as a Source for Staging Details

The tragedies provide remarkably few particulars about dramatic production. There is no mention of settings, costumes, blocking (stage positions and movement of actors), or character descriptions — not even notations of entrances and exits. There is no punctuation, no division between words, and usually no indication of which character speaks a particular line. The imagination of the translator must be relied upon to supply descriptions of the settings, costumes, masks, and stage business. The translator is also left with the task of rationalizing the corruptions and inconsistencies that have crept into the scripts over two millennia.[15]

There are a few reasonably certain aspects of staging that can be gleaned from the tragedies: (1) a tabulation of roles verifies the statement of Aristotle and others that the number of actors assigned to a tetralogy was limited to three (see chapter 9); (2) the near-total absence of onstage fights and killings, a stock-in-trade of later dramatists, indicates with reasonable certainty that there existed a rule forbidding onstage violence; (3) an offstage area probably existed, since the three actors needed to enter and exit, if for no other reason than to change costumes; (4) at least one practical open-and-close door was a necessity, but its location cannot be determined from the scripts.

Aside from these general requirements, there are some specific needs for individual plays. Some examples: the Watchman in *Agamemnon* is usually assumed to be stationed above the orchestra;[16] a minimum of one chariot is necessary for Agamemnon's triumphant homecoming; Orestes must leave a lock of his hair on a tomb or altar; Medea needs some device, presumably wheeled, to carry off her dead children; Philoktetes requires a cavelike opening for his residence; Euripides' lines specify that Elektra live in a rude shepherd's hut, that her hair be unkempt and greasy, and that she wear garments of ragged and dirty homespun. A few other necessaries can be found in the tragic scripts, but they fall far short of justifying the elaborate scenic embellishments supplied by most modern translators. Such descriptions may add to the reading pleasure of the scripts, but one should keep in mind that they are modern additions.

The comedies suffer from the same lack of stage directions and visual descriptions as tragedies and satyr plays. But, unlike the long-ago-and-far-away environment of most tragedies, the comedies were concerned with contemporary events. Aristophanes' plays constitute a gold mine of detail for the historian, furnishing information on costuming, machinery, tragic playwrights, and acting. They also tell us what Athenians ate and drank, something of their digestive processes, their clothing, their couplings, their attitudes toward the gods, women, foreigners, and each other. If one defines realism as *Kleinmalerei*, the creation of a picture from many little details, comedy is much more realistic than tragedy.

The travestied use of tragic machinery for comic purposes provides a clearer picture of tragic staging than the tragedies themselves. Agathon, pictured as a transvestite playwright, is wheeled out on what must have been the near-fabled *ekkyklema*, a device widely hypothesized as a means for revealing the bodies of those slain offstage in the tragedies. Similarly, the *mechane*, apparently utilized by Euripides for ascents and descents of the gods in his tragedies, finds clear applications in the comedies: Socrates, in *The Clouds*, is suspended above ordinary mortals in some kind of flying device; in *Peace*, Trygaeus journeys through the heavens on the back of a gigantic dung beetle; in *The Birds*, Iris probably "flies" on and offstage; and Perseus may fly in *Thesmophoriazusae*.

The door suggested by the tragedies is an absolute necessity in such comedies as *The Wasps*, where Philokleon must be barricaded inside his house. Details of tragic costuming come from the comedies: in *The Acharnians*, the actors provide a cataloguing of the many tattered, disreputable costumes worn by Euripidean heroes — implying that other tragedies used a more dignified kind of attire.

WRITINGS ABOUT THEATRE

Aristotle

Aristotle remains an essential primary source, not only because he is the sole surviving commentator on the drama from the Classic Age, but also because he possessed considerable powers of observation and analysis. However, three caveats should be considered when using his writings as source material: (1) although a member in good standing of that hallowed group known as "the Ancients," Aristotle lived at some chronological distance from the events about which he wrote — *The Poetics* is no closer to the origin of tragedy than are present writings to the beginnings of American Colonial theatre; (2) there are questions about the authenticity and accuracy of the manuscripts, and *The Poetics* may be Aristotle's lecture notes, jottings by one of his students, or even the writings of someone else; (3) Aristotle's bent is essentially literary, not theatrical.

The last point needs elaboration. Henry Arthur Jones, a turn-of-the-century British playwright with literary aspirations, saw the written drama and the producing theatre as two constantly warring factions:

> The drama and the theater are so often antagonistic to each other; they so often differ, if not in their body and essence, yet in their interests and aims, that we should always be careful to distinguish between them. Much of our confusion of thought in matters dramatic and theatrical arises from our constant habit of using the words *drama* and *theater* as if they were always interchangeable terms. . . . I have often said that the greatest enemy of the English drama is the English theater.[17]

Aristotle would have agreed with Mr. Jones, for both belong to that group of critics, commentators, and writers who have slight regard for the process of play production or for the persons engaged in its practice: to coin a word, they may be described as "dramateurs,"[18] individuals who hold in high regard *only* the literary aspects of the theatre.

This emphasis upon the literary values of the plays is changing. Recently, J. R. Green wrote that he was attempting to discover something of the audience's view of the theatre and the reader can, if he or she likes, contrast it with the view of the literary scholars which has the text as its central focus. For scholars approaching ancient drama from that angle, the poet's creativity is the important thing, and although scholars nowadays take some account of the performance aspects of the texts, in the history of scholarship it has traditionally meant study of the texts and appreciation of its literary value almost regardless of whether it was ever performed.[19]

Plato, Aristotle's teacher at the Academy and forty-five years his senior, undoubtedly nourished his pupil's disdain for the theatre. While pupil and teacher differed in their attitude toward the dramatist, neither showed much regard for the actor. While Plato treated playwrights such as Euripides and Agathon with respect, he banned actors from his *Republic*. Ion, a *rhapsode* (reciter of Homer), is the closest to an actor encountered in Plato's writings, and he is introduced only as a buffoonish straw man for Socrates to demolish. According to Jonas Barish,

> The actual theater, as known to Plato and practiced by his contemporaries, can in the last analysis be allowed no virtue. It has corrupted society, and it continues to symbolize the evils which have led to Athens' downfall. And Plato's hostility toward it is destined to become the cornerstone of an anti-theatrical edifice that is only now, after two and a half millennia, finally crumbling.[20]

Aristotle, as Plato's disciple, shows a comparable aversion to theatre folk. "Why," he asks rhetorically, "are Dionysiac artists generally bad characters? Is it because they have least share in the theory of wisdom since most of their life is spent in arts which they practice for a living, and because so much of their life is spent in incontinence and some in dire straits?"[21] In *The Poetics*, he quotes an argument advanced by the Peloponnesian Dorians that "their word for the outlying hamlets is *coma*, whereas the Athenians call them demes — thus assuming that comedians got the name not from their *coma* or revels, but from their strolling from hamlet to hamlet, *lack of appreciation keeping them out of the city*" (emphasis added).[22]

Aristotle's "spectacle" was the major element of theatre that kept 14,000 Athenian spectators in their seats. Comprised of all the visual elements of performance, spectacle makes theatre different from other art forms; nevertheless, Aristotle had little use for spectacle, calling it "the least artistic of all the parts [of tragedy], having the least to do with the art of poetry." With an apparent sneer he adds that "the getting-up of the spectacle is more a matter for the costumer than the poet." He then proceeds to drive the final nail into the coffin of producing theatre: "The tragic effect is quite possible without a public performance and actors."[23] This hallmark sentiment of the dramateur is echoed down the centuries by such literary critics as Samuel Johnson, who wrote that "a play read affects the mind like a play acted."[24] T. S. Eliot, himself an occasional playwright, found that the stage actually interfered with his enjoyment of the drama: "I know that I rebel against most performances of Shakespeare's plays because I want a direct relationship between the work of art and myself."[25]

Demosthenes and Other Orators

Contemporary with Aristotle are the writings of fourth-century orators, valuable but often neglected sources. Disapproval is always couched in more concrete terms than praise, and while references to theatre are mostly tangential, these quarrelsome "lawyers" tend to be quite specific in making their points. Aeschines, for example, supplies a scrap of information about audience arrangements when he speaks disapprovingly of "cushioned seats of honor" being reserved for Philip's Makedonian ambassadors.[26]

Demosthenes' orations are of special interest because he was once involved with theatrical performance as sponsor/producer (*choregos*) of his tribe's entry in the dithyrambic competitions. (His birth and death dates, incidentally, coincide exactly with those of Aristotle.) Demosthenes seems to have spent the greater portion of his public life fighting with one person or another about the details of specific events, with the result that his comments about staging, audiences, festival arrangements, actors, musicians, and the stresses of competition supply often-missing details of theatre production.

Vitruvius and Pollux: Sources of Misinformation

The theatrical writings of Vitruvius (first century BCE) and Pollux (second century CE) should carry this label: "Warning! Take with extreme caution: grievous error may result from misuse." Vitruvius' often-parroted misstatement about the evils of a southern orientation for theatres (discussed in chapter 7) is a glaring example. These writers show neither any particular affinity for the theatre nor informed knowledge of how it operated. Both wrote at least as far removed in time from Classical Greece as are present-day scholars from the theatre of Shakespeare — and with much less source material to draw upon. Both are inclined to dogmatic and unsubstantiated pronouncements.

Vitruvius was a Roman architect and military engineer who lived during the first century BCE. He is known mainly from *De Architectura*, the only surviving work on ancient architecture and engineering; part of this was his own writing, but he also drew upon other sources. The rediscovery of his writings during the Italian Renaissance resulted in a reactivation of the long-unused system of Roman aqueducts, lending substantial authority to his writings.

Pollux, a lexicographer, was born in Egypt and resided in Athens for most of his life; he held a chair of rhetoric there sometime after 178 CE. Certainly he had the advantage of being able to consult materials no longer available; but in evaluating his writings, some consideration should be given to the corruption introduced by later writers: the extant manuscripts "are derived from four incomplete, abridged, and interpolated copies from an early epitome possessed (and interpolated) by Arethas, archbishop of Caesarea, c. A.D. 900." [27]

These authors still maintain membership in the exclusive Ancients Club, that group of writers from the past whose words are often treated as Holy Writ. Increasingly, however, the dicta contained in Vitruvius' *De Architectura* and Pollux's *Onomasticon* are viewed with skepticism. Researchers nowadays have grown a little gun-shy about citing the writings of the Roman architect and the late-Greek lexicographer; there is a tendency to take more of a cafeteria approach with these "authorities," picking and choosing what does and does not represent "truth." Selections from this ancient cafeteria seem currently based upon the following three factors.

1. Vitruvius and Pollux are cited where a minimum of confirming archaeological evidence has been uncovered. Thus, only *two* verifiable sets of "Charon's steps" ascending from underground to the orchestra level, one at Eretria and the other recently uncovered in the fourth-century theatre at Argos, have been offered as "proof" that Pollux was correct in making these steps a standard feature of Greek theatres rather than occasional oddities. Reasoning from Pollux, early scholarship misinterpreted storm drains at Sikyon and Segesta as examples of Charon's steps. There are indications of two below-grade stepped entrances into the orchestra at Corinth, but their nature and purposes are not clear; the Theatre of Dionysos shows no evidence of a man-sized tunnel in the bedrock lying just beneath the orchestra.

2. Statements of Vitruvius and Pollux have sometimes been adopted with-

out reflection. For example, Vitruvius' injunction against south-facing theatres has been frequently cited without checking to see whether this statement had a basis in fact. (Chapter 7 considers this matter of orientation.)

3. Their pronouncements are invoked when they agree with what researchers regard as sound theatrical practice. "Common sense" demands an
Up Center (UC) entrance into the acting area, but there is no archaeological
evidence to confirm this. (Chapter 5 discusses this matter of entrances.)

Other Writers

An assortment of authors from the past recorded occasional comments
on plays, performances, actors, and audiences. Athenaeus (second or third
century CE) is probably the most useful of these. His *The Learned Banquet*
(*Deipnosophists*), is the multivolume account of a symposium-style dinner
which lasted several days. In this work, educated participants engage in a
leisurely discussion of life, love, literature, politics, social customs — and
the theatre. Included are excerpts from historians, poets, and playwrights of
times past, many unknown outside the pages of this work. The author seems
to have had no axe to grind, so these rambling conversations supply apparently unbiased theatrical detail.

Mention must be made of "The Scholiast," the collective name for
a group of scholars from various ages who deposited marginalia upon
the preserved manuscripts. These library-bound scholars lacked an understanding of the working theatre. Their scribbled comments concern mainly
textual matters; while of interest in solving problems of exegesis, these an-
notations provide little enlightenment for anyone investigating problems of
theatrical production.

The *Suda* or *Suidas* should also be mentioned, as this work is often included among the works of the Ancients. This monkish lexicon-encyclopedia
was compiled at the end of the first millennium of the Common Era. The
few theatrical references contained therein should be treated as more fantasy
than fact.

Further sources of misinformation are the *Vitae*, very brief biographies
of the playwrights; they are of uncertain antiquity and disputed authorship.
Lefkowitz has done a rather complete job of showing that most of the material contained in these *Lives* is based upon inferences drawn either from
the plays themselves or from an enshrinement of the caricatures contained
in the comedies.[28] The cautionary label affixed to the theatrical writings of
Pollux and Vitruvius should also be applied to the *Vitae*.

CONCLUSION

Many so-called truths about the Greek theatre have been created by over-reliance on questionable evidence. Too often contradictory testimony has been disregarded, particularly when it conflicted with established dogma. Written evidence about the Greek theatre should be treated with a degree of skepticism, keeping in mind the prejudices, limitations of viewpoint, and chronological distance of the authors from their subject — as well as the sometimes dubious authenticity of the evidence. Many opinions of present-day writers are tempered by nineteenth-century classicists who felt that one of their major tasks was to refute any evidence conflicting with the recorded views of any member of the Ancients Club.

NOTES

1. Oliver Taplin, *The Stagecraft of Aeschylus*, 436.

2. The course of Athenian drama may have been affected by other city-states: Epicharmus of Syracuse is sometimes regarded as the father of Old Comedy.

3. James Diggle, *Euripides*, 45.

4. Most of the surviving scripts were first performed at the City Dionysia, although some of the comedies are from the Lenaia. There is the general presumption that all of the plays received productions in Athens, but this is not wholly verifiable; Euripides' *Iphigenia at Aulis* may have been first produced at the court of Archelaus in Makedonia.

5. Donald William Lucas, "Euripides," in *The Oxford Classical Dictionary* (1970).

6. Bruno Snell, "Zwei Töpfe mit Euripides Papyri," *Hermes* 70 (1935): 119–120. The other missing five plays from this sequence are *Theseus, Thyestes, Ino*, and two *Hippolytus* plays.

7. G. Zuntz, *An Inquiry into the Transmission of the Plays of Euripides*, 110.

8. See Bernard Knox, "Euripidean Comedy," in *Word and Action*, 250–274.

9. Richmond Lattimore, ed., *The Complete Greek Tragedies, Euripides I*, v.

10. 1261–1263; William Arrowsmith translation.

11. Mary R. Lefkowitz, *The Lives of the Greek Poets*, 105–106.

12. Whitney J. Oates and Eugene O'Neill, Jr., eds., *The Complete Greek Drama*, 2:480.

13. Euripides' semicomic *Alkestis* was substituted at one contest for the prescribed satyr play. While its grave-humor is less farcical than either *Cyclops* or the partially preserved *Trackers*, the inclusion of a drunken god (Herakles) guaranteed that the audience would be laughing, even if not as heartily as they usually did at the buffoonish choruses of ithyphallic satyrs.

14. The practice is probably much older; an attempt to provide a light afterpiece in 1599 is recorded by Thomas Platter, a Swiss traveler to London. He wrote that after a perfor-

mance of *Julius Caesar*, the actors "danced together admirably and exceedingly gracefully, according to their custom, two in each group dressed in men's and two in women's apparel" (Ernest Schanzer, "Thomas Platter's Observations on the Elizabethan Stage," *Notes and Queries* [November 1956]: 465). Schanzer argues that the entire company performed in a "Longs for four" country-dance (466).

15. Most of these "improvements" were added to the plays in the century immediately following their composition. They resulted from tinkerings by scribes and scholars and from actors seeking to fatten their roles. As copies were made from copies, there were also simple errors in transcription. See Denys L. Page, *Actors' Interpolations in Greek Tragedy*.

16. See Oliver Taplin, *The Stagecraft of Aeschylus*, 276–279.

17. Henry Arthur Jones, "Introduction to Brunetière's 'Law of the Drama,'" in Barrett H. Clark, ed., *European Theories of the Drama*, rev. ed. (New York: Crown Publishers, 1947), 460.

18. See Clifford Ashby, "The Playwright and the 'Dramateur,'" *Dramatists Guild Quarterly* (Winter, 1998): 14–20.

19. J. R. Green, *Theatre in Ancient Greek Society*, xii.

20. Jonas Barish, *The Anti-theatrical Prejudice*, 28.

21. Aristotle, *Physical Problems*, 956b11–15. Questions have arisen about Aristotle's authorship of this work, but the antitheatrical sentiments expressed are consonant with his other writings.

22. Aristotle, *Poetics*, 1448a35–1448b1.

23. Ibid., 1450b17–29.

24. Samuel Johnson, "Preface to Shakespeare," in Clark, *European Theories of the Drama*, 189.

25. Quoted in Oliver Taplin, *Greek Tragedy in Action*, 172.

26. Aeschines, "On the Embassy," 111.

27. *Oxford Classical Dictionary* (2nd ed.), s.v. Pollux.

28. Lefkowitz, *The Lives of the Greek Poets*. Appendices include translations of the *Vitae*.

2

THE LIMITS OF EVIDENCE II
Physical Remains

A host of researchers study the physical remnants of Classic Greek theatre. Four overarching disciplines, archaeology, architecture, art history, and epigraphy, supply the bulk of information that is useful to anyone concerned with how the theatre operated in the fifth century. At times, specialists in such fields as numismatics, micromorphology, papyrology, geoarchaeology, dendrochronology, and others supply further data.

Each area of specialization has differing interests, concerns, approaches — and limitations: the archaeologist is typically engrossed in artifacts uncovered at a particular site; the architect's preoccupation with aesthetics, architectonics, and decoration seldom leads to consideration of such plain, roofless structures as theatres; the art historian's concerns are with aesthetics, composition, subject matter, dating, and attribution, but seldom with how the figures on the vases relate to actual performances; the epigrapher pieces together jigsaw puzzles of stone, clay, and metal, guessing at missing parts where necessary. Each specialty, while seldom immediately concerned with the subject, contributes evidence useful in the piecing-together of theatre history.

THE THEATRES

Roughly 200 Greek theatres have survived to the present day in various states of preservation and alteration. They lie scattered east–west from Marseilles to Afghanistan, north–south from the Mediterranean coast of Africa

FIGURE 3. *Pergamum: sockets for wooden stage supports.*

to the Balkans.[1] While the final stone remains can be dated with some certainty, it is nearly impossible to determine when these sites were first used for performances or what the original shape may have been.

Archaeological teams have explored many of these theatres, digging down through many layers of habitation, positioning and cataloguing shards, seeds, coins, bones, and anything else brought to light. Eventually, after years of study, a final excavation report is published. Written in a daunting array of languages, these reports appear in an assortment of technical journals and monographs issued by publishers of varying size and prominence. At times, these reports seem nearly as difficult to unearth as were the original sites.

Unfortunately — at least from a modern perspective — no Greek site has been preserved in the manner of the Vesuvius-entombed theatres at Pompeii and Herculaneum; all were modified by later ages. The theatre at Delfi, for example, was rebuilt by Eumenes II, king of Pergamum, in 159 BCE and was further altered during the Roman occupation. The earlier, airier, wooden *skenai* known mainly through vase paintings have left no physical traces beyond some stone sockets into which wooden posts or beams were inserted, as at Pergamum (fig. 3). All surviving structures are built of stone, and only two of these can be dated earlier than the mid–fourth century BCE: Thorikos and Argos, both straight-rowed theatres from the fifth century, might have been known to Aeschylus, Sophocles, Euripides, and Aristophanes; even these had scene houses built of wood.

Caution must be exercised when extrapolating backward in time from stone structures to wooden ones; the fifth-century theatres were mainly products of the carpenter, not the stonemason. For the modern reader/researcher, visualizing original productions in wooden theatres is difficult, given the near-universal tendency to view the Classic Age as occurring in Jeffersonian Greek-Revival architecture. Modern stage settings for tragedies are usually based upon thick, closely spaced stone columns and massive lintels, rather than the thin columns and wooden beams of the fifth century.

VASES, STATUES, TERRA-COTTAS, WALL PAINTINGS, AND MOSAICS

Pictorial evidence from the Classical Age began to receive serious attention with the 1920 publication of Margarete Bieber's *Die Denkmaler zum Theaterwesen im Altertum*.[2] Although only a few vases from the fifth century deal even tangentially with actors, many from the fourth century and later provide evidence that wooden scene houses (*skenai*) were not immediately replaced by stone at the end of the fifth century. While these vases are receiving increasing study, any application is complicated by the painters' greater interest in creating a pleasing design than in recording a particular moment of theatrical history. Not uncommonly, architectural elements are subtracted to avoid cluttering the composition; characters are added, subtracted, and rearranged for effective picturization. As a result, vases frequently depict dramatic moments never seen in the theatre — not unlike present-day publicity photos. Other vases are not theatrical, showing mythological scenes only vaguely influenced by stage representations, while still others may be versions-of-versions painted by artists lacking a background in either theatre or mythology; one is reminded of Mexican *retablos* showing Jesus studded with St. Sebastian's arrows.

Most of the theatre scenes are painted on burial offerings found in Magna Graecia; sorting out the theatre-related scenes from those memorializing the dear departed is difficult. The majority are clearly funerary offerings with conventionalized temple/tomb structures framing a representation of the honoree, often with his horse and armor. A few show spring- or well-houses associated with mythological figures.

Whether the subject is theatrical, mythological, or a representation of the recently departed, the vases show similar framing structures of widely spaced, thin, polelike columns supporting wooden horizontal beams that span much greater distances than would be possible using thick stone lintels. Visually, the differences between wood and stone are startling; light, airy carpenter-built structures seem scaled for habitation by human beings.

The translation of these user-friendly wooden structures into monumental stone leads to an interesting speculation: the change in scale may have altered the physical size of the actor. Beginning in the second century BCE, tragic performers were made larger-than-life by the addition of high shoes, elaborate headdresses, and padded costumes. This effort to monumentalize the actor may have been an attempt to bring the human figure, now dwarfed by the stone setting, into scale with the background.

The wooden theatre structures of the tragic vases are almost identical to the temple/tomb/well-house structures shown on the vases. On all of these, usually four but occasionally six or even eight thin columns support a low pitched roof (fig. 4). Most of the clearly theatrical depictions are not very realistically portrayed, with both male and female figures appearing as mythic personages rather than masked actors.

FIGURE 4. *A typical* naiskos *setting:* Alkestis. *Courtesy of the Antikenmuseum Basel und Sammlung Ludwig, Inv. S 21.*

The framing structure, now usually labeled *naiskos*, typically serves to house multiple scenes jumbled together. What these buildings represent is arguable. The following identifications have been offered: (1) one of the projecting wings (*paraskenia*) of the *skene*; (2) the UC door of the *skene*; (3) a portable piece of stage scenery which might sometimes be placed in front of the UC door.

Comic scenes are much more easily identified as theatrical. Those from the Greek mainland as well as the so-called *phlyakes* vases from southern Italy depict figures in grotesque masks, impressive phalluses, and padded jerkins, with outsized bellies and posteriors (fig. 5). Staging elements of these comic scenes are more complete; some show practical doors, some a raised stage with access stairs, and a few have figures seated in windows on the second level. In many ways, the comedy *skene* would appear to be a different building from that used in tragic performances.[3]

Only a few of the statues are pertinent; these are Roman copies of the originals, mainly portraits of famous playwrights. While no stone-carved statues depict actors in performance, many tiny terra-cottas of actors have

FIGURE 5. *The comic stage: Heracles and Auge. Photo courtesy of the Soprintendenza alle Antichità, Sicily, from a drawing by R. Carta.*

been unearthed, often mold-made for wide distribution. Almost all are the masked and padded figures of comedy; they clearly depict a grossly exaggerated comic style that must have been popular.

Occasional Roman wall paintings may relate back to the fourth or fifth centuries. A well-known Roman mosaic shows an aged playwright or chorus master giving backstage instructions to members of a satyr chorus (fig. 6). These depictions, usually thought to be copies of Greek originals, are of some use in re-creating theatrical conditions from several centuries before.

EPIGRAPHIC EVIDENCE

"Written in stone" implies a degree of unchanging permanence, but does not guarantee that the original inscription was totally accurate: witness the Parian Stone, which until recently enjoyed about the same degree of unquestioning acceptance that Moses' tablets received from the Children of

FIGURE 6. *Backstage at a satyr play. Courtesy of the Museo Nazionale, Naples.*

Israel. Fragments from this marble stele, found in 1627 on the island of Paros, have provided dates for many historic events which took place in Athens, some seventy sea miles distant. On this stone, the date of 534 BCE is recorded as the first known instance of a tragic contest in Athens, with Thespis as the victor. However, the inscription was not cut until 264–263 BCE, some 270 years after these fabled events. Currently, a cloud of very reasonable doubt swirls around the date of 534, one which had hitherto been enshrined among the very few fixed points in the ever-evolving study of Greek theatre. Rush Rehm writes that "based upon a probable misreading of an inscription on a marble slab called the Marmor Parium . . . the conclusion that the Great Dionysia was instituted in 534 BC by the tyrant Peisistratus hardly seems secure."[4]

Generally, however, inscriptions provide valid recordings of events. Contest dates, play titles, names of playwrights, *choregoi*, actors, records of victories in the tragic and comic contests, and construction details of theatres are known from stone writings unearthed in various parts of the Greek world. Inscriptions from the island of Delos, for example, provide third-century BCE information about the painted panels (*pinakes*) inserted between columns of the *skene*.

CONCLUSION

Considerable information about the Greek theatre has been assembled in individual caches by scholars working independently; unfortunately, there is no central clearing-house where the fruits of these studies are brought together, so the theatre researcher must often hunt for them in obscure, not readily accessible locations. The pursuit, although often difficult, is frequently rewarding.

There is more to theatre research than time spent in the study and the library. On-site study, even if of necessity conducted in the later stone theatres, provides insight into production problems and performance situations encountered by the playwrights, actors, and technicians of ancient times. Pilgrimages to excavation sites sometimes result in the discovery of details omitted from written studies.

Fieldwork also leads to the less arduous but equally rewarding task of wandering through the world's museums and libraries: astonishing numbers of Greek artifacts have found homes in minor as well as major collections scattered around the globe. Every small museum has a painted pot or two (roof tiles in the tiny museum at Iato are stamped *theatron*, presumably to prevent theft), and locating a previously unknown (at least to you) figure, vase, or book in some out-of-the-way repository provides an unexpected joy to smooth the potholes of back-road travel.

NOTES

1. The most complete listing of theatre sites is contained in a large, little-known "photo atlas" titled *Athletic-Cultural Archaeological Sites in the Greco-Roman World* by Russell L. Sturzebecker (503 Owen Road, Westchester, PA 19380). Both written and published by Sturzebecker, a sports historian, the volume covers, almost incidentally, the ancient theatres in addition to his chief interest, sports arenas. His catalogue ranges from England and northern Europe to Syria and Jordan. The author, having visited and photographed these sites, takes time to supply travelers' directions to all of these numerous locations. This book, still in print, contains a great deal of useful information — despite shortcomings in archaeological and bibliographic detail. In 1993 Leslie du S. Read was "in the final stages of

completing a history and guide to ancient theatre sites," but his work has not yet appeared. See "Social Space in Ancient Theatres," *New Theatre Quarterly* 36 (November 1993): 316.

2. Bieber also used artwork in her efforts to re-create Greek costumes. See her *Griechische Kleidung*.

3. See Alan Hughes, "Comic Stages in Magna Graecia: The Evidence of the Vases," *Theatre Research International* 21 (Summer 1996): 95–107.

4. Rush Rehm, *Greek Tragic Theatre*, 15.

3

THE SHAPE OF THE ORCHESTRA

A History and Critique

The Greek theatres which first became known to scholars had partially circular orchestras with a wrap-around hillside viewing area: The theatres at Priene, Sikyon, Eretria, and the Theatre of Dionysos at Athens were among the first excavated, and all exhibited this part-circular pattern.

However, it was the theatre at Epidauros, also excavated in mid-nineteenth century, that had the greatest impact upon early researchers; extolled since the time of Pausanias as an example of beauty and architectural harmony, Epidauros became an early model for the quintessential Greek theatre. The orchestra here was a complete circle defined by a stone curbing, and this led to the speculation — which was ultimately elevated to a conclusion — that the full circle was *the* primitive orchestra shape, that *all* primordial theatres had been constructed with totally circular orchestras. Further conjecture established a neat and orderly progression of orchestra shapes: first the full circle, then a gradual paring-down of the portion nearest the scene house until the semicircular orchestra of the Roman theatre resulted.

Casting about for an ancestor of the complete circle, classicists seized upon the ancient threshing circle, still a ubiquitous sight throughout the Greek world. Here again a logical progression was posited: first, happy peasants linking arms and treading out the grain in the threshing circle, with song and dance lightening the monotony of their task; second, spectators assembling on a hillside to watch the merry threshing crew; third, soloists (actors) added to what by now had become a performance.

This scenario dominated most Greek theatre studies until the early part of the twentieth century. It not only served to explain the remains which had been uncovered, but also predisposed archaeologists to discover a similar pattern in new excavations. The circular shape became the hallmark of the ancient theatre; any excavated structure that lacked a rounded orchestra could not possibly be a theatre.

There are some fundamental objections to this pattern of development.

1. Theatrical dance tends toward a rectangular pattern, not a circular one. "Where dancing is concerned, the most natural setting for it is a circular space," wrote O. A. W. Dilke in 1948;[1] given such a sweeping dictum, one envisions dancers swirling around a circular orchestra. A group of musicians sitting at an altar is usually added at the hub of this circle, providing an inward focus for the dancers; this embellishment is somewhat supported by the writings of Vitruvius and Pollux.

While the dance-in-a-circle chorus is still a commonly held concept, it does not acknowledge the essential difference between folk and theatrical dance. Round dancing is not intended for exhibition; its participants dance for their own pleasure, not for that of spectators. If onlookers are present, they usually surround the dancers on all sides. Dance-as-performance is another matter: as soon as important spectators, priests, princes, or elders assemble in a certain location, the dancers turn toward them, and the center focus is abandoned. The dance has now become a presentation done for others.

There is little evidence of round dancing in Classical times. Vase paintings usually picture dancers in-line, often with hands linked, typically following a god, a priest, or a flutist. If contemporary folk patterns are to be evoked in determining the dances of the past, it should be noted that present-day Greek dance is serpentine, not circular; a leading dancer guides followers through various seemingly random patterns, much like the figures on the vases.

Line dancing does not fit into a circular arena. Sir Arthur Evans, after excavating the "theatral area" at Knossos, organized a performance in that rectangular space using some of his Cretan laborers; he found that "the sinuous meandering course of the dancers was in fact quite appropriate to the Knossian tradition."[2] For many years, the Dora Stratou dancers appeared each summer in a varied program of Greek dances on the slopes of the Pnyx; they performed in a rectangular space.

2. The threshing circle is an unlikely progenitor. Threshing in ancient times was much more easily accomplished by teams of cattle or donkeys driven around the circle, not by dancing peasants.[3] There is little evidence to suggest that, in the Classic period, monotonous thresh-walking was done by people when beasts were available. Xenophon has a dialogue participant say, "'Then you know this much, that draught animals are used in threshing?'"[4]

One curious but unremarked fact is that while threshing floors are paved with stone, Greek orchestras remained dirt-floored until Roman times. If one is descended from the other, the stone covering of the threshing circle would have been retained for the orchestra. Further, as Alan Hughes remarks, the unyielding surface of the threshing floor causes performance problems: "Stone or concrete can give an actor shin splints."[5]

3. *There is very little archaeological evidence of complete-circle orchestras, and what there is occurs too late to fit into any developmental sequence.* The complete-circle theatre at Epidauros was built at the end of the fourth century, long after other theatres had part-circle orchestras. Recently, a French team has uncovered a Hellenistic full-circle stone-curbed orchestra at Argos, which had been partly hidden beneath a later Roman scene house.[6] Aside from these two examples, both on the Peloponnesos, there is very little physical evidence supporting the primal circle. Vitruvius provides the only written support: he configures his Greek and Roman theatres around a complete circle, but in both of these intrusive scene houses cut into the circles.

4. *Wood lends itself to straight-line, not curved construction.* The principal theatres known to Aeschylus, Sophocles, Euripides, and Aristophanes were wooden. While large blocks of soft stone such as marble, limestone, or poros can be sculpted into whatever shape is desired, trees can only be used as boards, beams, and columns. Benches or bleachers made of wood could only be straight, and this would have dictated a straight-fronted performance area.

5. *Discovery of a growing number of straight-line performance areas indicates that the rectangle/trapezoid rather than the circle may be the ancestral orchestra form.* Although rectangular performance areas were known in the nineteenth century, it was not until Carlo Anti published his treatise, *Teatri greci arcaici da Minosse a Pericle* that serious attention was given to them. In this book, Anti formulated the hypothesis that the oldest theatres had rectangular or trapezoidal orchestras. His work was largely devoted to a re-examination of known nonconforming performance structures, previously dismissed as either out-of-the-mainstream aberrations or rude, countrified places of assembly having nothing to do with the development of theatre.

A legend has arisen that Anti's book "met with almost universal rejection,"[7] but a survey of reviews and comments indicates a reserved but generally favorable judgment. George R. Kernodle wrote admiringly of Anti's theories in the *Educational Theatre Journal*,[8] as did William A. MacDonald in the *American Journal of Archaeology*.[9] The greatest measure of praise, however, came from Margarete Bieber, who stated in the *American Journal of Philology*: "The reviewer agrees with most of the theories of Anti. . . . The book is full of interesting and challenging observations, and the main thesis [the rectilinear orchestra] is convincing and fruitful."[10] In a longer review in *Art Bulletin*, Bieber stated unequivocally, "Anti is right [that] until the end of the fifth century the Greeks used rectangular, not rounded auditoria."[11]

The influence of Anti's theories is quite evident in the later edition of Bieber's *The History of the Greek and Roman Theatre* (2nd edition revised and enlarged, 1961). Anti's reconstruction of a trapezoidal theatre in Athens' precinct of Dionysos is included, along with two other possible versions (56), and Bieber's rectangular ground plan for the Lenaian theatre "is based on the investigations of Anti" (70). However, her absolute belief in Anti's theories had wavered by the publication of this second edition: she wrote there that an early rectangular orchestra in the Theatre of Dionysos "is unlikely, as in most theatres it is circular" (55).

A few well-known scholars came down firmly in opposition to Anti's attempt to place these structures within the pattern of theatrical development. Chief among them was Arthur Pickard-Cambridge, who regarded the straight-line structures at Rhamnous and Ikaria as "two small country places where the builders did what local conditions required."[12] He dismissed the rectangular theatre at Thorikos as "the town's public place."[13] Anti's book suffered from inadequate fieldwork. World War II had kept him virtually imprisoned in his native Italy, forcing a reliance on library research and a handful of accessible Italian sites, most notably the one at Syracuse. When freed from wartime restrictions, he began fieldwork in Greece in 1955; illness intervened, and he found it necessary to entrust his notes to Luigi Polacco, a former student.

Nuove ricerche sui teatri greci arcaici appeared in 1969 under the joint authorship of Anti and Polacco. Two European quarterlies published generally favorable reviews,[14] but the book was ignored by British and American journals. Despite some interesting, even startling, observations on the theatres at Chaironeia, Oropos, Argos, Corinth, and Athens, *Nuove ricerche* is today virtually unknown.

Twenty years after Anti's death, the long-awaited monograph *Il teatro antico de Siracusa* appeared under the authorship of Polacco and Anti, with the collaboration of Maria Trojani. This handsome and well-illustrated two-

FIGURE 7. *Phaistos: setting for a choral performance.*

volume work laid to rest any lingering doubts about the originally trapezoidal shape of the orchestra at Syracuse.

MINOAN/MYCENEAN PERFORMANCE AREAS

The first straight-line performance sites are pre-Greek, dating from the
beginning of the second millennium BCE: well-defined Cretan locations at
Phaistos, Knossos, Gournia, and Mallia, together with sketchy remains at
Poliochni (on Lemnos), all possess squared-off performance areas with adjacent risers.[15] Phaistos (fig. 7) is clearly intended for choral performance:
well-defined stone pathways provided a ceremonial entrance for the performers, while spectators stood or sat on the adjacent flat portions. A similar arrangement is found at Knossos (fig. 8). Whether spectators occupied
the stepped locations or the flat area is debatable: as noted previously,
Arthur Evans placed his audience on the risers, which could accommodate
only a very small audience and are not pitched steeply enough to allow
spectators to see over those in front. More likely, the steps were occupied by
a chorus which had proceeded down stone pathways (fig. 9) similar to those
at Phaistos.

FIGURE 8. *Knossos: the performance area.*

FIGURE 9. *Knossos: the entrance pathway.*

FIGURE 10. *Lato: eighth-century steps.*

EIGHTH-CENTURY GREEK SITES

"Theatral areas" (a term coined by Evans) at Amnisos, Drero, and Lato offer evidence that the Minoan configuration was not abandoned by later ages. Lato (fig. 10), the largest of these, has a series of risers of seemingly random heights (7 to 16 inches), fronting a large courtyard or agora; the question again arises as to whether performers or spectators occupied the stepped area. It was probably used as seating; the irregular height and the spacing of the seats are similar to those shown in the sixth-century vase fragment by Sophilos, which has spectators both standing and sitting (fig. 11).

THE CLASSIC PERIOD

Lato has another straight-line performance area, this one from the fourth century; because of the odd conformation, photographs (fig. 12) are not as illustrative as the ground plan shown in chapter 4 (fig. 22). Facing a rectangular performance terrace 100 feet long and 50 feet wide are the following: (1) an exedra, a U-shaped bench, 40 feet in length and 15 feet deep; (2) ten to eleven rows of stepped seating around 50 feet in length; (3) six

FIGURE 11. *A vase by Sophilos. From* Monuments et mémoires, Fondation Eugène Piot. *Paris: PUF, 1933.*

FIGURE 12. *Lato: the fourth-century performance area.*

to ten steps cut into a rounded rock, apparently serving as a viewing area for an altar situated at the edge of the terrace (the base still remains). The steps near the altar are greatly eroded and probably predate the performance area.

According to the excavators, "there is scarcely any doubt that the lower terrace, the exedra and the seating form a coherent ensemble fulfilling a precise function."[16] Just what this function might be is problematic: some sort of processional, paradelike presentation is a likely possibility.

SITES ON THE PELOPONNESOS AND IN BOEOTIA

Theatres at Isthmia, Tegea, Oropos, and Corinth show evidence of having been originally constructed on a straight-line pattern, although later alterations have made them circular. Perhaps the most conclusive evidence of rectilinearity is found at Chaironeia and Argos. The ground plan (fig. 13) of the former shows the remains of an early straight-rowed *theatron* extending outside the curved rows of the later theatre; these are still discernible. At Argos, a later Roman *odeion* has been carved from living rock on the former site of a large straight-rowed theatre from mid-fifth century (fig. 14); large straight-rowed portions extending outside the smaller Roman structure are clearly visible (fig. 15). Seating around 2,500, the remaining rows, apparently

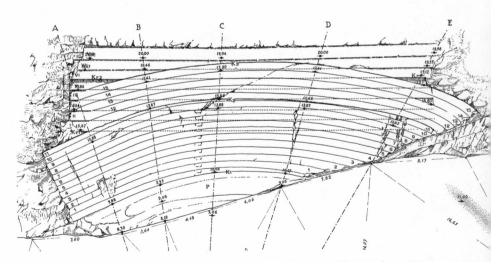

FIGURE 13. *Chaironeia: the ground plan. From Carlo Anti and Luigi Polacco,* Nuove ricerche sui teatri greci arcaici.

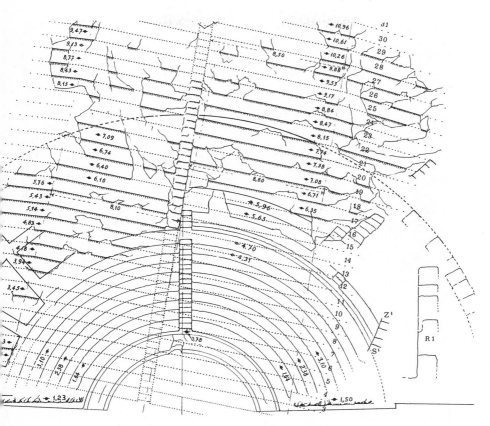

FIGURE 14. *Argos: ground plan of the fifth-century theatre and overlaid Roman* odeion. *From Anti and Polacco,* Nuove ricerche.

straight, have a slight curvature not apparent to the naked eye, a characteristic shared with the seating at Thorikos (discussed later).[17]

MAGNA GRAECIA

The trapezoidal drainage ditch surrounding a primitive orchestra of the theatre at Syracuse (fig. 16) offers clear evidence of early rectilinearity. Morgantina (fig. 17), like Chaironeia and Argos, has several straight rows remaining at the back of the now-curved seating. Alongside the huge and thoroughly Romanized theatre at Locri, a few straight rows are cut into the hillside; these may be the remains of a sixth- or fifth-century theatre, but they might also have been part of a *bouleuterion*. Anti found

FIGURE 15. *Argos: straight rows remaining above the later Roman* odeion.

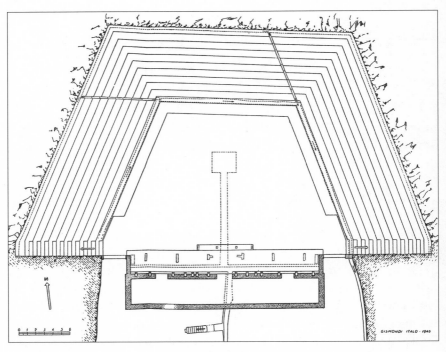

FIGURE 16. *Syracuse: the ground plan. From Carlo Anti,* Teatri greci arcaici.

FIGURE 17. *Morgantina.*

quadrilateral elements in the foundation wall lying below the Roman theatre at Catania.[18]

NORTH AFRICA AND THE ISLANDS

Rock cuttings at the North African city of Cyrene indicate that a rectangular theatre may have preceded the later Roman one. On the island of Thera (Santorini), a circular theatre has been fitted into a rectangular plot of land (a not uncommon practice for Hellenistic city planners). Anti claims that the original plan was rectangular, and O. A. W. Dilke, no advocate of rectilinearity, admits that "Anti may be right in thinking that the walls under the lateral *kerkides* [seating sections defined by stairways] belong to an earlier rectilinear *cavea*."[19]

STRAIGHT-LINE THEATRES IN ATTICA

The well-defined remains of five rectilinear theatres lie within thirty miles of Athens: Thorikos, Ikaria, Rhamnous, the Amphiaraion at Oropos, and Trachones. (The theatre of Munychia may also be rectangular, but its remains still lie beneath the modern city of Piraeus.)

FIGURE 18. *Thorikos.*

Thorikos is the oldest surviving Greek theatre on the Continent, dating from the sixth century (fig. 18). A long straight section of slightly curved seating (as at Argos) faces a rectangular performance area; additional seating wraps around the sides.

Trachones, discovered in 1973 (fig. 19), lies near the Athens airport not more than four miles from the Athenian "high city," the akro + polis. The orchestra is definitely rectangular, measuring 24.6 feet x 50.2 feet. Seats enclose three sides of the orchestra; the six thrones of Hymettos marble can be dated to the end of the fourth century.[20]

THE THEATRES OF CLASSICAL ATHENS

The Agora

Ancient sources place an "orchestra" somewhere in the vicinity of Athens' central market area. In all likelihood this was a multipurpose performance area, probably the site of the two celebrated collapses of the wooden seating (*ikria*), in 499–498 and again in 465 BCE. The nature of these seats is uncertain; Dilke concludes that they were no more than benches for sitting or standing.[21] But to have occasioned recorded comment upon their

FIGURE 19. *Trachones.*

failure, something more calamitous than the breaking of a bench or two was involved. I have talked to former tent show performers, now advanced in years, who remember vividly the screams of spectators caught in the bone-crunching collapse of a bleacher section; this kind of catastrophe would have caught the attention of the chroniclers.

Further, Dilke's randomly placed benches, whether for sitting or standing, would block the view of those behind. Bleachers are more likely; given the nature of wood, they would define a rectangular playing area.

The Lenaion

Anti posits a rectangular orchestra for the Lenaion, with bleacher seating for 2,000 on one side. Based upon his reading of Aristophanes and a few discernible rock cuttings, he locates this theatre, devoted mainly to comedy, on the slopes of the Areopagus, near the shrine to Dionysos en Limnais and not far from a swampy area where frogs cried their "brek-kek!" Bieber used Anti's ground plan in reconstructing a first production of *The Frogs* (fig. 20), and MacDonald felt that Anti had identified "the precinct with a good deal of plausibility."[22] Pickard-Cambridge was predictably full of doubt: "The whole of this reconstruction is very hazardous."[23]

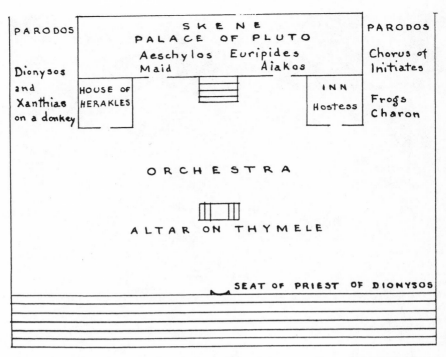

FIGURE 20. *Lenaion: a possible performance ground plan, according to Bieber. From* The History of the Greek and Roman Theatre, *copyright Princeton University Press, 1939, 1961: renewed 1989 by Princeton University Press.*

The Theatre of Dionysos

Needless to say, the orchestra of this most celebrated of Greek theatres is a scholarly minefield. The few stones remaining from the Classical Age have been interpreted in numerous ways, none of them completely convincing. Literary and artistic sources, like the archaeological remains, are tantalizingly indefinite.

Anti triggered his share of explosions when he stepped into this treacherous arena. Working from library sources in Italy, he mistakenly interpreted a dotted line running between a long-abandoned well from the Mycenean period and a manhole from the Classical Age as a drainage ditch for a straight-fronted orchestra. This "ditch" exists only on paper; William Bell Dinsmoor speculates that it was created when Ernst R. Fiechter, "in a forgetful moment," drew a dotted line connecting the manhole and the well.[24]

Some genuine evidence of rectilinearity did emerge at the Theatre of Dionysos after Anti's work was published. Scavenged rock sections used in construction of a later (and quite actual) drain proved to have been originally part of a straight-line seating arrangement. Unearthed were a total of seven slabs of two types, and Dinsmoor used one variety of these to fashion a stone bench for the first row of officials; he then employed the remaining ones as vertical supports for wooden seats behind the front row.[25]

No one has quarreled with Dinsmoor's reconstruction to this point, but here interpretations diverge: he uses his seating to form nine straight-rowed sections (*kerkides*) which bend polygonally around the standard part-circular orchestra;[26] Elizabeth Gebhard, on the other hand, feels that "it would perhaps be simpler to suggest that the original wooden seats, arranged in parallel rows, were partly replaced in stone without changing their alignment."[27] Gebhard's solution is plausible, but the Hellenistic remains of theatres at Mycenae, Vergina, and Orchomenos-in-Boeotia offer support for Dinsmoor's version: in these theatres, only the first row is of curved stone, with the remainder apparently having been wooden sections arranged in the polygonal pattern that Dinsmoor outlines.[28]

CONCLUSION

When rectangular theatres first came to light in the late nineteenth century, they caused considerable consternation among archaeologists imbued with the concept of theatrical circularity. Walter Miller, excavating at Thorikos in 1896, could not understand why the builders did not make the theatre circular from the start,[29] and Pickard-Cambridge, as late as 1948, argued (mistakenly) that the contour of the hillside dictated Thorikos' rectangular shape.[30] B. Staïs, searching at Rhamnous in 1891 for a "théâtre canoniquement disposé," thought that he had discovered part of a school.[31] Carl D. Buck began excavating at Ikaria in 1880 and found to his astonishment that, if his plans were made to include a conventional dancing circle, "the seats for the priests come in a straight line across the center of the orchestra."[32] When W. Dörpfeld began his work on the Theatre of Dionysos, "He was looking for evidence of the original orchestra circle [and he found it] in three small sections of polygonal masonry, . . . one of which he assigned to the perimeter of the early orchestra and thus provided material evidence for the idea of a primary orchestra circle."[33] Excavators were operating on the principle that theatres were constructed with a standard circular shape, convinced that actors required this configuration in order to put on a play; therefore, anything lacking the requisite form could not be used for dramatic purposes.

The absence of a discernible progression caused further distress for researchers. Coupled with the out-of-sequence appearance of the fourth-century complete-circle orchestra at Epidauros, further chronological confusion was occasioned by discovery of straight-rowed theatres at Thorikos (sixth century), Argos (fifth century), and Morgantina (fourth century).

A half-century has now passed since Anti first broached his revolutionary hypothesis. Scholarship, moving with predictably glacial speed, has gradually begun to assimilate the concept of the primal rectangular/trapezoidal orchestra. Oscar Brockett writes in the latest edition of his *History of the Theatre* that "an increasing number of archaeologists believe that early theatrical spaces on the Greek mainland were square or rectangular." [34] While far from a ringing endorsement, this statement in a general history (Brockett keeps abreast of current scholarship) does indicate a shift in outlook; the idea of theatre starting from a rectangle rather than a circle has forced investigators to rethink previously drawn conclusions.

A final judgment may never be reached. The dispute presently remains part of the continuing effort to solve what Sidney Markman has called "the almost insoluble problems dealing with the Greek theatre building"; [35] but, at the very least, in Anthony Snodgrass' words, "even when the rightness of the new explanation is less than demonstrable, the doubts cast on the old can be salutary." [36]

NOTES

1. O. A. W. Dilke, "The Greek Theatre Cavea," *Annual of the British School at Athens* 43 (1948): 128.

2. Sir Arthur Evans, *The Palace of Minos*, 3:585.

3. See Jack R. Harlan, *The Living Fields: Our Agricultural Heritage*, 228.

4. Xenophon, *Oeconomicus*, 8.3.

5. Alan Hughes, "Comic Stages in Magna Graecia: The Evidence of the Vases," *Theatre Research International* 21 (1996): 102.

6. J.-Ch. Moretti, "Argos: Le théâtre," *Bulletin de Correspondance Hellénique* 112 (1988): 716–717.

7. Elizabeth R. Gebhard, *The Theatre at Isthmia*, xvi.

8. George R. Kernodle, "Recent Scholarship on the Greek Theatre," *Educational Theatre Journal* 3 (1951): 130–131.

9. William A. MacDonald, review of *Teatri greci arcaici, American Journal of Archaeology* 53 (1949): 412–414.

10. Margarete Bieber, review of *Teatri greci arcaici, American Journal of Philology* 53 (1949): 449–450.

11. Bieber, review of *Teatri greci arcaici, Art Bulletin* 31 (March 1949): 63.

12. A. W. Pickard-Cambridge, review of *Teatri greci arcaici*, *Classical Review* 62 (1948): 125.

13. Ibid.

14. See reviews by V. Verhoogen, *Revue Belge de Philologie et d'Histoire* 49 (1971): 223; and Michael Maas, *Gnomon* 46 (1974): 95–97.

15. A more complete site-by-site consideration can be found in Clifford Ashby, "The Case for the Rectangular/Trapezoidal Orchestra," *Theatre Research International* 13 (Spring, 1988): 1–20.

16. Pierre Ducrey and Olivier Picard, "Recherches à Latô IV: Le théâtre," *Bulletin de Correspondance Hellénique* 95 (1972): 527.

17. René Ginouvès, *Le théâtron à gradins droits et l'odéon d'Argos*, 81.

18. Carlo Anti, *Teatri greci arcaici*, 122–125.

19. Dilke, "The Greek Theatre Cavea," 188.

20. Olga Tzahou-Alexandri, "Anaskafi theatrou stois Trachones Attikis," *Praktika* (1980): 64.

21. Dilke, "The Greek Theatre Cavea," 147.

22. MacDonald, review, 414.

23. Pickard-Cambridge, review, 127.

24. William Bell Dinsmoor, "The Athenian Theater of the Fifth Century," in *Studies Presented to David Moore Robinson* (St. Louis: Washington University, 1951), 312.

25. Ibid., 328.

26. Ibid., 325. This ground plan is reproduced in Bieber, *History*, 58.

27. Elizabeth R. Gebhard, "The Form of the Orchestra in the Early Greek Theatre," *Hesperia* 43 (1974): 434.

28. An early report on the remains of the theatre at Mycenae mentions "round stones *in situ* which could have served as bases for wooden uprights." These stones are no longer visible at the site. See O. A. W. Dilke, "Details and Chronology of Greek Theatre Caveas," *Annual of the British School at Athens* 45 (1950): 38.

29. Audrey Eunice Stanley, "Early Theatre Structures in Ancient Greece: A Survey of Archaeological and Literary Records from the Minoan Period to 388 B.C.," 94.

30. Pickard-Cambridge, review, 125. Dilke writes: "The theory that the slope of the hill rendered a rectilinear cavea easier to construct, and that only the sides had to be curved, must be abandoned in view of Cushing's discovery that the natural shape of the hill was semicircular" ("Details and Chronology," 28).

31. Jean Pouilloux, *La Forteresse de Rhamnonte*, 73.

32. Carl D. Buck, "Architectural Remains in Ikaria," *Papers of the American School of Classical Studies at Athens* 5 (1886–1890), 65–66.

33. Gebhard, *The Theatre at Isthmia*, xv.

34. Oscar G. Brockett, *History of the Theatre*, 31.

35. Sidney D. Markman, review of *Teatri greci arcaici*, *Classical Journal* 44 (January 1949): 279.

36. Anthony Snodgrass, "Archaeology," in *Sources for Ancient History*, ed. Michael Crawford (Cambridge: Cambridge Univesity Press, 1983), 138.

4

WHERE WAS THE ALTAR?

After centuries of study, there is general agreement that the City Dionysia of fifth-century Athens involved an animal sacrifice to the god Dionysos and that this event took place in the theatre before the beginning of the play competition. The usual assumption has been that this sacrifice was offered upon an altar situated at the center of a circular orchestra.

This placement fits well with the theory that tragedy grew from a dithyrambic chorus dancing in a circle around the altar of Dionysos. But now that the dogma of the originally circular orchestra has been questioned, some attention must also be given to the location of the altar, a supposedly standard piece of theatre furniture. This chapter discusses the origin of the concept of a centrally located altar; examines the literary, artistic, and architectural evidence which relates to altar placement; and suggests that an altar placement on the perimeter of the orchestra makes better theatrical sense and is more in accord with the evidence.

ORIGINS OF THE CONCEPT

The concept of a central altar grew out of readings of "the Ancients," mainly Greek or Roman writers of the Christian era — although playscripts, writings of Aristotle, inscriptions, and scraps of information from Classic sources were also studied. As early as 1827, at a time when archaeology was still the exclusive property of the Society of Dilettanti, Philip Wentworth Buckham wrote:

In front of the orchestra, opposite the middle of the scene, there stood a high place with steps like an altar of the same height as the stage, called

Thymele. This was the place where the chorus assembled when it was not singing, but was a spectator of the action and a participator in it. . . . The *Thymele* was in the centre of the whole building; all distances were measured from it, and the semicircle of the amphitheatre was described about this point. It was therefore pregnant with meaning that the chorus, which was in fact the ideal representative of the spectators, had its place exactly in the spot where all the radii drawn from their seat converged to a point.[1]

This belief gained support from two discoveries made at the end of the nineteenth century: one is a round stone located in the middle of the circular orchestra at Epidauros, and the other a round hole at the center of the orchestra at Athens' Theatre of Dionysos. Because of the predisposition toward a central location, these seemingly opposite pieces of evidence, a stone and a hole, were both construed as confirmation of a central altar.

A. E. Haigh in *The Attic Theatre*, published in 1889, stated the orthodox opinion: "The altar probably stood in the very centre of the orchestra. This was the arrangement in the earliest times, when the drama was still a purely lyrical performance; and it is not likely that any alteration was made afterwards." He based his conclusion on two pieces of misinformation.

The evidence supplied by the theatres of Epidaurus and the Peiraeeus [*sic*] is distinctly in favour of the same view. In each of these theatres there is a circular hole in the centre of the orchestra. The only plausible explanation of the holes is that they were intended for the reception of small stone altars. On the above grounds therefore it seems reasonable to conclude that the position of the altar was in the centre.[2]

Haigh is in error: the theatre at Epidauros has a small stone rather than a hole in the center of the orchestra, while the second-century theatre at the harbor of Athens has neither hole nor stone. Pickard-Cambridge corrected these errors in his 1907 revision of Haigh's work.[3]

W. Dörpfeld and E. Reisch confirmed the central placement of the altar in 1896 with the publication of *Das Griechische Theater*.[4] Since they lacked evidence of an actual altar from the Theatre of Dionysos, they "borrowed" a second-century rectangular altar from the Agora area, an imposing structure with multiple dedications to Aphrodite Hegemone, the Demos, and the Graces.[5] Sitting on a *bema* (platform) measuring 5.4 feet by 5.1 feet, it had a chopping surface of 4.5 feet by 3.2 feet.[6] This interpolated altar, although lacking any connection with a theatre, provided a model for many later theatre reconstructions.

Questions were raised about the central location of the altar in the year following the appearance of the Dörpfeld and Reisch book, and a lively debate ranged through the pages of the German journals as late as 1924.[7] Arguments centered upon three areas of dispute: the etymology and definition of the word *thymele*; references to altars in the playscripts, together with possible requirements for altars in the stage business; and archaeological evidence concerning the presence of an altar in the theatre.

Thymele was variously interpreted to mean an altar, a building foundation, the center section of the orchestra, or the orchestra entire. The various arguments were supported with usages that ranged from Pratinas, writing at the beginning of the fifth century BCE, to Hesychius, an Alexandrian lexicographer of the fifth century CE. Not surprisingly, these discussions produced more heat than enlightenment.

Examination of the physical evidence also proved inconclusive. When an adherent of the unorthodox viewpoint stated that only one theatre altar had ever been found — and it was not at the orchestra center (Priene) — Dörpfeld replied that there were "indications" of altars at Athens, Epidauros, Priene, Thorikos, Pergamum, and Delos. Dörpfeld was willing to concede that, after the introduction of a raised stage, the altar probably migrated to an upstage position, but this minor retreat was about the only detectible change in anyone's basic belief during this quarter-century dispute.

Basically, all these arguments were advanced to support two differing visualizations of Greek tragedy. One camp saw an active performance, with an orchestra cleared of encumbrances and musicians relegated to a platform or station at the side. No central altar dictated a circular movement for the chorus; neither did it obstruct sight lines, nor provide an obstacle to such stage business as the maneuvering of Agamemnon's chariots.

The orthodox view favored a more symmetrical, ritualized, and relatively static performance: musicians sat on the central altar base at the feet of the soloists/actors, and the chorus danced about them in a circular pattern, much as harvesters were presumed to have trodden out grain on circular threshing floors. Dörpfeld, spokesman for the canonical view, was supported by the weight of past scholarly tradition — and also by his standing as heir to Heinrich Schliemann's excavations at Troy. His authority prevailed; although objections continued to be raised from time to time, they attracted little attention. The dogma of the central altar resting at the *Mittelpunkt* of a circular orchestra had been proclaimed and accepted.

LITERARY EVIDENCE

The plays themselves provide remarkably little testimony about location, although altars are frequently mentioned. Many scripts require places of sacrifice, presumably tombs and/or altars; in *Ion*, Creusa uses the altar of Apollo as a sanctuary much in the comic manner of later Plautine slaves.

The proposal has been offered that a permanent, centrally located altar could have served for religious sacrifice at the start of festivities and then functioned as a stage property, dropping its dedication to Dionysos and temporarily becoming the altar of Artemis, Agamemnon, or whatever god/personage was specified by the script. However, this practice would have reduced the religious significance of the altar. Perhaps more importantly, a central location would have forced the composition of a monotonous stage picture around this dominating centerpiece.

Nondramatic writing, all of it from much later ages, provides scraps of information — or, more usually, misinformation. Pollux, the second-century CE Greek lexicographer, writes of *two* altars:

> And the *skene*, on the other hand, is part of the actors' realm, but the orchestra, on which there is also the *thymele*, being either some sort of a raised platform or altar, is part of the realm of the chorus. And upon the *skene* (also the *agyieus*) is situated an altar, the one in front of the doors and a table having sacrificial cakes, a table which is called a *theoris* or *thyoris*. The *eleos*, however, was the ancient table upon which, before the time of Thespis, someone getting on top of it answered the choral dancers.[8]

Some murky evidence is also provided by the *Suda*, which was put together at the end of the first Christian millennium; this lexicon/encyclopaedia drew upon texts of Homer, Sophocles, Aristophanes, and the amorphous *Greek Anthology*. The relevant passage offers more obfuscation than enlightenment:

> *Skene*: A stage is the middle frame of the theatre. The *paraskenia*, however, are the stages on either side of the middle frame. And in order that I may speak more clearly, after the stage and straight to the side-stages is the orchestra. And this is the place which holds up the base from the planks, from where the mimes perform. After the orchestra is the altar of Dionysos, which is called the *Thymele* [the following diagram is included in the text]:

beside this a person sacrifices, and after the "seat," the arena [literally, "place of dust"], which is below the ground floor of the theatre. Also scenic, which is upon the stage. Ever, O divine Sophocles, may the ivy that adorns the stage dance with soft feet over thy polished monument [the final sentence is taken from a poem by Erycias in *The Greek Anthology*].[9]

Vitruvius makes no mention at all of any altar in his writings on either the Greek or Roman theatre. Such an omission has no particular significance; Vitruvius also omits mention of *prohedria*, the stone seats of honor that were surely present in the theatres of his time. He does refer to the chorus by the Greek word *thymelici* (of uncertain meaning), but that is his only possible reference to the presence of an altar.[10]

In "The Altar in the Fifth-Century Theater," Joe Park Poe works painstakingly through the dramatic scripts and ancient lexicographers quoted above — without considering any of the archaeological evidence.[11] He concludes that, while there may have been property altars of varying sizes, there was also a permanent altar at an unspecified location. Basing his argument upon Pollux's use of the term *agyieus* in connection with altars (see the passage quoted above) and its relation to the worship of Apollo Agyieus, Poe posits that a "theatrical *agyieus*-altar stood on the [raised] stage . . . in plays in which the *skene* represented a house or palace. . . . The *agyieus*-altar's distinctive shape [a pointed column] argues strongly, if not conclusively, against the notion that the altar was a fixed, conventional theatrical property."[12] How an altar shaped like a tiny Washington Monument or Cleopatra's Needles could be used for sacrifice is not explained.

ARTISTIC EVIDENCE

Vases show that altars had many dramatic uses; the following ones are referenced by their numbers in A. D. Trendall and T. B. L. Webster, *Illustrations of Greek Drama*. On a simple level, altars were useful to painters (and presumably actors) as a place to sit (*Iphigenia in Tauris*, III.3.28) or even as a platform for standing (*Herakleidae*, III.3.20). Usually, the sitting pose is combined with the use of the altar as a sanctuary, a place where violence is forbidden. Orestes seeks safety in Delfi on the altar of Apollo (*Eumenides*, III.1,12); Alkemena finds momentary safety on an altar, but she is about to be driven off by a large fire lit beside her perch (III.3.6 – 8). Some altars are used for libation (*Aigeus*, III.3.3); one from *Iphigenia in Tauris* has a statue of Artemis sitting on it (III.3.29). Another, from Euripides' *Oineus*, apparently involves human sacrifice; a bound Agrios sits on the altar as Diomedes offers his grandfather, the aged Oineus, a sword to dispatch the evildoer.

Comedy scenes, long thought to picture regional farces of Magna Graecia, are increasingly regarded as representations of mainstream Greek comedy. Alan Hughes has identified for me thirteen comic vignettes involving altars, but almost all give little indication of placement on the stage. However, two of these altars are situated on a wooden stage: the "Bari Pipers" (*Comic Angels*, 14:11) and the "Heracles and Auge" pictured in chapter 2, fig. 5. All thirteen altars are particularized and apparently scene-specific; the two altars shown onstage are positioned to suit the action of the particular scene rather than being permanent architectural features of the theatre.

Two conclusions can be drawn from the tragic and comic vases: when altars are shown, they are involved in the action of the scene; and the altars are highly particularized, adding further doubt as to the existence of a standard stage altar.

In three-dimensional art, Bieber pictures four New Comedy slaves done in terra-cotta, all perched saucily and safely (for the dramatic moment) upon what appear to be small property altars.[13] These, like the altars shown on the vases, differ in detail one from the other; they do not suggest an in-situ theatre altar serving many plays.

ARCHITECTURAL EVIDENCE

Materials from the theatres themselves are more interesting than the vases and figurines; they provide a firmer basis for speculation. This evidence can be grouped under six headings: center holes and center stones (Dionysos, Epidauros, Argos, Eretria, Vergina); other possible emplacements in the orchestra (Philippi, Isthmia); emplacements near the orchestra (Thorikos, Lato, Morgantina); confirmed altars found in theatres (Priene); questionable altars found in theatres (Kephalos, Orchomenos-in-Arcadia, Butrinto); clearly inapplicable evidence (Corinth, Halikarnassos, the Kabirion near Thebes, the Asklepion at Pergamum).[14]

Center Holes and Center Stones

Both the round hole in the center of the orchestra at Athens' Theatre of Dionysos and its surrounding diamond-shaped marble flooring relate to the orchestra's use as a courtyard for a Christian basilica built into the roofed-over eastern *parodos* during the fifth century CE.[15] The function of this hole is not known. The center stone at *Epidauros* is definitely *not* the base for an altar, according to von Gerkan and Müller-Wiener: the diameter (2.4 feet) is too small for a foundation, and the center depression is too large to be a dowel hole. Moreover, round dowels are not found at Epidauros, and there is no casting channel (*Gusskanal*) which would have allowed for the introduction of lead to coat a connecting iron staple.[16] The authors conclude that the stone served as a fixed point from which various measurements like seating radii could be taken during the many years of construction. They suggest also, with somewhat less plausibility, that it might also have been a marker used by the performers to maintain spacing.[17]

Argos, Eretria, and Vergina, theatres dating from the fourth and third centuries, have similar stones at the center point of a circle from which seat rows and the orchestra perimeter could be laid out. Manolis Andronikos maintains that the center stone at Vergina was an altar base; in an imaginative reconstruction based upon no evidence, he argues that this small stone, apparently salvaged from some earlier structure, either "stood in the same place in an earlier theatre, or it belonged to some shrine of Dionysos and hence was consecrated as the altar of a new theatre."[18]

Other Possible Emplacements in the Orchestra

Two theatres hint at altars in the orchestra, although neither is placed at the center. *Philippi* is a largely Romanized theatre uncovered by a French excavation team in 1927. Built originally in the fourth century during the reign of Philip II, the present remains do not provide much enlightenment about its original condition. The theatre was last used for animal baiting, and the original stones have been moved and reshaped to provide a separation between beasts and spectators. The writing, photographs, and ground plan of the original report are difficult to interpret, but apparently show a space of unspecified size 6 feet (1.83 m) on the audience side of the orchestra, among the large Roman paving stones which cover the orchestra. According to the report, this "rectangular emplacement is reserved, without doubt, for the *thymele*."[19] Nothing at the site confirms this "emplacement."

At *Isthmia*, the hardpan orchestra surface of the early fourth century theatre shows a rectangular cutting 4.4 feet by 2.2 feet with a depth of 1.3 feet. It is situated 6 feet from the *proskenion* and slightly to one side of the center line of the theatre. The excavator, Elizabeth Gebhard, no advocate of a central altar, admits somewhat grudgingly that "its depth and shape suggest that it was cut to receive a foundation block or blocks, perhaps to support an altar. . . . Shards from the first century A.D. found in the bottom indicate that the foundation was removed at the time of the first Roman remodeling."[20]

Emplacements Near the Orchestra

Of three theatres suggesting altar locations outside the orchestra, *Thorikos* presents the strongest case. This well-known theatre dating from the sixth century is situated in a mining town some 37 miles from Athens; it is the oldest surviving theatre on the Greek mainland. The site was abandoned by Roman times (perhaps because of flooding), thus escaping later remodeling. A foundation generally regarded as an altar base measuring 4.9 feet by 13.1 feet sits on the side of the rectangular orchestra (fig. 21). According to the Belgian excavators, there is "a strong impression that both the temple [of Dionysos, located Stage Left (SL)], the eastern rooms and the altar [both Stage Right (SR)] constituted part of the fifth-century architectural unit."[21]

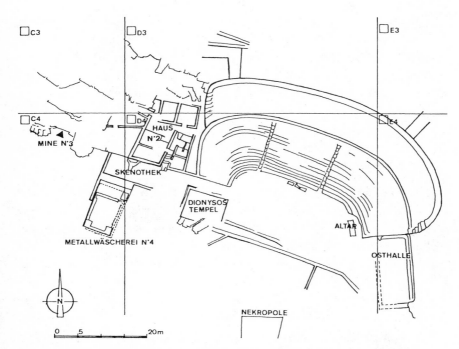

FIGURE 21. *Thorikos: the ground plan. From H. F. Mussche et al.,* Thorikos 1965: Rapport préliminaire.

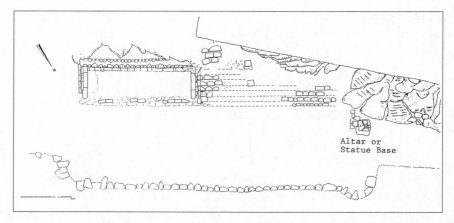

Altar or
Statue Base

FIGURE 22. *Lato: the ground plan. After P. Ducrey and O. Picard, "Recherches à Latô IV: Le théâtre."*

The fourth-century performance area at *Lato*, in eastern Crete, was pictured previously in chapter 3, fig. 10. The base for a small altar or statue sits at the edge of the oldest portion of the rectangular "orchestra" (fig. 22).

The theatre at *Morgantina*, located in the Sicilian interior, has, according to Eric Sjoquist, "on each side of the stage . . . a long low podium seemingly without any structural connection with the [fourth-century] building. I suggest that they were altars. The god to whom they were dedicated was, in this case, Dionysus, as can be seen from the dedication inscription of the theater itself." [22]

Confirmed Altars Found in Theatres

The second-century BCE altar at *Priene*, the first theatre altar ever to be uncovered (1895–1898), remains the only one that is completely verifiable (fig. 23).[23] Positioned at the edge of the orchestra in line with the stone *prohedriae*, this seeming exemplar had no impact upon the prevailing theory that altars sat in the middle of the orchestra. An imposing structure 5.9 feet long, 3.0 feet deep, and 4.5 feet high, this altar has a working surface measuring 4.4 feet by 3 feet, making it suitable for the sacrifice of a ram, goat, or pig, but somewhat cramped for the body of a bullock, the animal traditionally associated with Dionysos. However, the inscription on the altar leaves no doubt as to the god for whom sacrifice was intended: "Pythotimos, son of Athenopolis, is the one presiding for Dionysos." [24]

FIGURE 23. *Priene: the altar.*

Questionable Altars Found in Theatres

Orchomenos-in-Arkadia (fig. 24) has in its present condition two *prohedriae*, Down Left (DL) and Down Center (DC), with a small columnar altar sitting between them; all are placed on stone bases near the outer circumference of the orchestra. Another base, Down Right (DR), indicates that a third *prohedria* at one time completed a symmetrical arrangement. According to a recent archaeological report, this altar is inscribed to Omonia (Harmony or Concord),[25] but no inscription can be discerned on the battered altar presently sitting there (fig. 25). The white marble benches outside the perimeter of the orchestra are inscribed "Epigeneos, the one presiding for Dionysos,"[26] attesting to the theatre's principal dedication.

Two pieces of evidence cast serious doubt upon the validity of this altar's placement: there is no sign of a balancing emplacement between the DC and DR thrones; and the original excavation report of the French School in 1914 makes no mention of an altar.[27] Its presence was first noted in the report of a Greek reexcavation in 1973. This opens the possibility that the altar, like one at Corinth (discussed later), was placed in the theatre by the early excavators because someone felt that the theatre needed an altar and happened to have this one available.

Reports on the theatre at *Kephalos*, situated on the island of Kos, note the

FIGURE 24. *Orchomenos-in-Arkadia.*

FIGURE 25. *Orchomenos-in-Arkadia: the altar.*

FIGURE 26. *Butrinto: the altar.*

presence in situ of a small round marble altar dedicated to Dionysos. This small theatre with only six rows of seating was excavated by an Italian team in 1928;[28] according to the report, the altar sat in the middle of the first row of seats. However, no photographs are extant, and the present location of the altar is unknown. Since the theatre shows no evidence of an emplacement for an altar, this raises the possibility that it may have been installed among the seats at a later time, perhaps by Roman or Byzantine hands. Curiously, an altar of suitable size sits outside the museum at Kos with a dedication to a person named "Dionysios."

Butrinto, in Albania, has a small altar placed rather casually at the SL corner of the *theatron*; Peter Robert Franke calls it "the theatre altar."[29] It is a crude, seemingly unfinished piece still showing comb markings (fig. 26), with nothing to identify it as either theatrical or Dionysian. Original excavation reports by an Italian group do not mention an altar, making its presence in this thoroughly Romanized theatre more than a little suspect.

Clearly Inapplicable Evidence

A white marble altar stands in the middle of the orchestra at *Corinth*; it is decorated with garlands and bulls' heads (fig. 27), and guidebooks published in several languages call this "the theatre altar." However, the earliest

FIGURE 27. *Corinth: the altar.*

photographs of the theatre excavation, begun in 1925, show an orchestra unobstructed by any furniture, and the publication makes no mention of an altar. Later photographs (excavation was largely completed by 1929) record the presence of the altar, but offer no explanation for its mysterious appearance in the theatre.[30]

Henry S. Robinson, a former director of excavations at Corinth, examined the altar at my request and writes the following:

> The altar which has been placed in the orchestra is that published in *Corinth II*, no. 192, and Fig. 95 on p. 123.[31] Apparently the exact provenance of the altar was not recorded, but it was presumably found in the area of the theatre — one cannot be more precise. It is a not uncommon altar type and it might have stood in the Greek orchestra; but the floor of the Greek orchestra, along with that of Early Roman times, was removed in late remodeling of the theatre (*Corinth II*, 8). It is therefore difficult to be certain that this particular altar (or any other) stood in the Greek orchestra.[32]

Very likely, some person unknown, feeling that every theatre requires a central altar, located this possible candidate in the course of excavation and placed it in the orchestra. Thus, archaeological evidence was manipulated to fit the stereotype.

The theatre of *Halikarnassos*, in the Turkish town of Bodrum, was well preserved as late as 1815; after that date it was plundered for building materials, much as the nearby tomb of Mausolos was used to construct a Byzantine fortress at the water's edge. Unfortunately, no drawings of the original ruins have been uncovered; the present theatre, of undetermined authenticity, was reconstructed during the reign of Kemal Atatürk. An obviously modern stone object resembling a sarcophagus but presumably intended as an altar was placed at the downstage edge of the orchestra. There is no inscription, and nothing has been learned about its origin.

The Kabirion near Thebes was not intended for play performance; the orchestra is almost totally filled by the base of what must have been an enormous altar, which presumably figured in the rites of this highly secretive cult. Very little is known about the Kabiri; children were involved as participants, and, interestingly, the benches are the lowest of any in Greece, the equivalent of primary school seats. The enormous size of the altar would make an Athens-type play nearly impossible.

The Asklepion at Pergamum includes a small theatre with a rather plain and uninscribed altar in the DC position (fig. 28); it is definitely Roman (second century CE). The present theatre was probably built on the site of

FIGURE 28. *Pergamum: the Asklepion altar.*

an earlier Greek theatre, part of a complex of buildings surrounding the Asklepion established around 350 BCE. The general arrangement of the theatre is certainly suitable for dramatic presentation, and Alice M. Robinson speculates that it may have been used for religious dramas as well as healing ceremonials.[33] However, the Roman date of the altar and a near-certain use in healing ritual place it outside the limits of the present discussion.

CONCLUSION

Pollux's *Onomasticon* and the *Suda* are the chief authorities for the central placement of the altar; their statements cannot be verified. As stated earlier, neither source exhibits a special knowledge of theatre or an understanding of production problems. Their confusing pronouncements are subject to varying interpretations.

The plays themselves confirm that altars were a necessary stage property; vase paintings and figurines show the use of altars in the plays, but only the two comic vases discussed earlier give some sense of placement. Most of the pertinent evidence is archaeological, but not all of this evidence is necessarily pertinent. The center stones found in four theatre orchestras are misleading; almost certainly these were building benchmarks, not altar bases. The hole currently present in the Theatre of Dionysos relates to the Christian era, not the Golden Age of Greece.

Of the remaining pieces of archaeological evidence, two excavations (Philippi and Isthmia) have emplacements which suggest an altar location within the orchestra circle, although not at the center, while three theatres (Thorikos, Lato, and Morgantina) have remains indicating that altars were placed at or near the perimeter of the orchestra. Three altars which have an in-situ appearance, Orchomenos-in-Arkadia, Kephalos, and Butrinto, are likely to have been introduced in post-Classic times and should be disregarded. Priene contains the only altar that was provably present in Hellenic or Hellenistic theatres.

A massive central altar such as that conjectured by Dörpfeld and Reisch would present a considerable problem during the four days of play production at the City Dionysia. An altar of any size placed in the center of the orchestra would force a monotony of stage picturization for the few productions where it could be incorporated and would be an obstacle for the remainder.

The preponderance of evidence suggests a location adjacent to the performing area. Priene's verifiably in-situ altar is found at the edge of the orchestra, and three firmly established emplacements are also in that location. A peripheral location would allow the altar a certain prominence throughout the entire festival without placing it in the very middle of *all* the dramatic action. In Athens, this would position the altar either in front of or behind the throne of the Dionysian priest, an appropriate location.

Conceivably, a portable altar might have been used, a stone or wooden affair rolled to the center of the orchestra for the initial sacrifice, then returned to a visible but less prominent position for the remainder of the festival. (Stone statue bases were sometimes hollowed out to make them easier to transport.) This is unlikely; until quite modern times when the Catholic Church began installing altars in the beds of pickup trucks for the use of peregrinating priests and their scattered parishioners, no example of a portable altar can be found. Holy images such as the chryselephantine statue of Dionysos were regularly paraded around, but altars in Classic times tended to be fixed and immovable.

On the other hand, there may never have been a major altar in the Theatre of Dionysos; one piece of evidence suggests the possibility that altars lying outside the theatre were used for preshow sacrifices. An oration by Andokides states that at the end of the fifth century, "the gateway of the theatre of Dionysus" was at the bottom of the hill somewhere below the orchestra;[34] and Bieber, without citing her sources, states that the audience

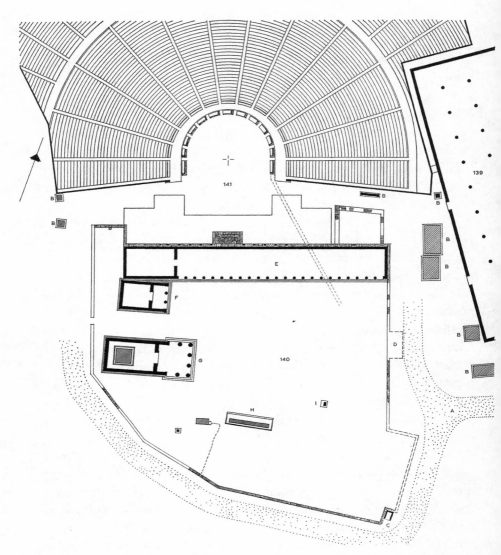

FIGURE 29. *Athens: the theatre and precinct of Dionysos. The altars are marked H and I. From John Travlos,* Pictorial Dictionary of Ancient Athens. *New York: Praeger Publishers, 1971. Reproduced with permission of Greenwood Publishing Group, Inc., Westport, Conn.*

entered the theatre through the *parodoi* alongside the orchestra.[35] This is initially puzzling, since there were excellent entrances into the theatre at the *diazoma*, the cross-aisle, which was actually a road leading to the Street of the Tripods on the east and the Agora on the west.

Logistical problems are encountered when considering the entrance of an entire audience through the *parodoi*. Assuming 14,000 spectators and an assembly time of one hour, over nineteen people per second would have had to pass through passageways only 8.2 feet (2.5 m) in width. Even doubling the assembly time, an unlikely prospect in terms of the length of the performances, does not eliminate the problem, which is further exacerbated by the possibility of ticket-taking. While the *parodoi* were undoubtedly used for a ceremonial procession, the entrances on the sides of the *theatron* must also have been opened to accommodate the arriving throng.

Why would a festival manager permit thousands of people to enter through the backstage areas and across the stage just as the tragedies were about to begin? One possible answer is that the multitudes were coming into the theatre from the sacred precincts of Dionysos, which lay directly behind the scene house of the theatre (fig. 29). This area contained *two* altars to Dionysos; if audience members entered from there, they would undoubtedly have witnessed a sacrifice on one or both of these altars, making a further offering in the theatre redundant — unless there was some special requirement for a brief purification ceremony within the theatre, probably involving nothing larger than a suckling pig and a very small altar.

There are some presently unanswerable questions. Why is there such a discrepancy in altar sizes — and what offerings were made? Assuming the correct placement of Omonia's altar at Orchomenos-in-Arcadia and the possibility of two altar emplacements at Morgantina, were altars to subsidiary deities found in theatres? Did all theatres possess permanent altars? If a sacrifice was necessary, how did it meld with the dramatic program?

But if further questions are raised, at least one answer emerges. Permanent altars in Greek theatres sat on the periphery of the orchestra; from this position, they could maintain a prominence without constituting a major obstacle to dramatic performance. There is very little evidence to support the presence of an altar in the middle of the orchestra.

NOTES

1. Philip Wentworth Buckham, *The Theatre of the Greeks*, 216.
2. A. E. Haigh, *The Attic Theatre*, 132.
3. Curiously, Pickard-Cambridge repeats this error in *The Theatre of Dionysus in Athens*. On p. 131, n. 3, he states, "Holes for the reception of altars are found in the centre of the orchestra in Athens and in Epidaurus," while on p. 147, n. 1, he writes, "The round stone in the centre of the orchestra at Epidaurus must also have been set for an altar."
4. W. Dörpfeld and E. Reisch, *Das Griechische Theater*.
5. John Travlos, *Pictorial Dictionary of Ancient Athens*, 79–81.

6. Dörpfeld and Reisch, *Das Griechische Theater*, 33–36.

7. The following papers, listed chronologically, are of interest in tracing this dispute: Carl Robert, "Zur Theaterfrage," *Hermes* 32 (1897): 421–453; Wilhelm Dörpfeld, review of "De certaminibus thymelicis," by Johannes Frei, *Deutsche Litteraturzeitung* 29 (20 July 1901): cols. 1816–1818; E[rich] Bethe, "Thymeliker und Skeniker," *Hermes* 36 (1901): 597–601; W. Dörpfeld, "Thymele und Skene," *Hermes* 37 (1902): 249–257; Erich Bethe, "Der Spielplatz des Aischylos," *Hermes* 59 (1924): 108–117. Of interest also is Erich Bethe, *Prolegomena zur Geschichte des Theaters im Altertum*. Although it is dedicated to Dörpfeld and Ulrich von Wilamowitz-Moellendorff, the author states that the book "is full of polemic against W. Dörpfeld and U. v. Wilamowitz" (vi). Unlocated but relevant is the dissertation by Johannes Frei, "De certaminibus thymilicis," Baseler Inaug.-Dissert. (Leipzig: 1900).

8. Pollux, *Pollucis Onomasticon*, ed. Eric Bethe, 237; translation supplied by Jon Cole.

9. Suidas, *Suidae Lexicon*, ed. Ada Adler, 4.375–376; translation supplied by John Thorburn.

10. *Vitruvius on Architecture*, ed. and trans. by Frank Granger, 1.283–291.

11. *Classical Antiquity* 8 (April 1989): 116–139.

12. Ibid., 137.

13. Margarete Bieber, *The History of the Greek and Roman Theatre*, 105.

14. David Wiles has recently written of three other altars which he says are found at Pergamum, Rhamnous, and Ikaria. I have been unable to verify their existence. See chapter 3, "Focus on the Centre Point," in *Tragedy in Athens*.

15. Travlos, *Pictorial Dictionary*, 549.

16. Armin von Gerkan and Wolfgang Müller-Wiener, *Das Theater von Epidauros*, 7–8.

17. Ibid.

18. Manolis Andronikos, *Vergina: The Royal Tombs*, 46. In another publication the author pictures an irregularly rectangular stone with only one finished vertical side and a square hole in the middle of the exposed surface. The square hole, presumably for a dowel, does not exist. See Manolis Andronikos, "Anaskafi Verginas," *Praktika* (1983-A): plate B.

19. Paul Collart, "Le théâtre de Philippes," *Bulletin de Correspondance Hellénique* 53 (1928): 96.

20. Elizabeth R. Gebhard, *The Theater at Isthmia*, 12.

21. H. F. Mussche et al., *Thorikos, a Guide to the Excavations*, 421. An earlier report notes, "The excavations of 1885 around the altar have made chronological interpretation of that element extremely difficult" (H. F. Mussche et al., *Thorikos 1965: Rapport préliminaire*, 93).

22. Eric Sjoquist, "Excavations at Morgantina (Serra Orlando), 1961: Preliminary Report VI," *American Journal of Archaeology* 66 (1962): 138.

23. The present altar dates from the beginning of the second century, presumably replacing one installed when the theatre was first constructed in the late fourth or early third century. See Ekrem Akurgal, *Ancient Civilizations and Ruins of Turkey*, 197–198.

24. Translation supplied by Peder Christiansen. A further inscription on a water clock in the theatre indicates that the priesthood may have been hereditary: "Athenopolis [listed on the altar as father of Pythotimos], son of Kydimoy, priest of Dionysos."

25. Georgios Stainhaouer, "Diamorphosis arkaiologikou horou Orchomenou," *Deltion* 29 (1973–1974): 301.

26. Translation supplied by Peder Christiansen.

27. G. Blum and A. Plassart, "Orchomène d'Arcadie: Fouilles de 1913," *Bulletin de Correspondance Hellénique* 38 (1914): 71–81.

28. Luciano Laurenzi, "Nuovi contributi alla topografia storico-archeologico di Coo," *Historia* 5(4): 625. See also Aldo Neppi Modona, *L'Isola di Coo nell'antichità classica*, 167.

29. Peter Robert Franke, "Albanien im Altertum," *Antike Welt* (1983): 11–65.

30. Richard Stillwell, *Corinth, vol. 2: The Theatre* (Princeton: American School of Classical Studies at Athens, 1952), 6–8 and figs. 1–2.

31. "Altar, circular (Fig. 95). ht. p.98m; diam. o.52m. Upper part worn and chipped all around. The foot consists of a plain torus surmounted by a cyma recta, with Lesbian leaf. The shaft carries, in high relief, four boukrania and swags or garlands" (ibid., 2:126).

32. Letter from Old Corinth, 18 November 1984.

33. Alice M. Robinson, "The Cult of Asklepius and the Theatre," *Educational Theatre Journal* 30 (December 1978): 530–542.

34. Andocides, *On the Mysteries*, in *Minor Attic Orators*, 1:371.

35. Bieber, *The History of the Greek and Roman Theatre*, 59.

5

THE SCENE HOUSE

The Dithyramb, Found Space, and the "Royal" Door

Theatre begins in space created for something other than theatre. As the last of the arts to flower, theatre does not emerge until other institutions are in place and functioning; only then do the actors begin to infiltrate the buildings and structures originally intended for other purposes. A major part of theatre history concerns the adapting of found space for dramatic use: medieval drama began in the church; the first proscenium theatre, the Farnese, was created inside a riding arena; the Elizabethan theatre was born in bullbaiting pits and innyards; Inigo Jones' elaborate masques were housed in banqueting halls; both the French and English used tennis courts for theatres; Max Reinhardt created a theatre within a *Redoutensaal*; Eugene O'Neill began on a New England wharf and graduated to a Greenwich Village stable; Richard Schechner housed his *Dionysos* in a parking garage. I directed my most recent productions in a vacant shopping center store, an abandoned movie house, a dance studio, and a large downtown building that once housed a men's clothier. How curious it is, then, that while tragedy is generally assumed to have evolved from some earlier performance mode, a usually unvoiced assumption maintains that the Greek theatre building was created specifically for the performance of tragedy. While it is true that *theatron* means "a seeing place," nothing specifies exactly what was to be seen.

Even the prototypical Greek theatre imprinted on most minds, a conception based upon stone remains from the fourth century, shows little design affinity for the production of tragedies. A row of columns obscures whatever upstage entrance might have been present; DR and DL double doors sitting behind columned porches serve little purpose in staging the surviving plays; and the orchestra — the "dancing place" — is too large to be filled by only three actors and some dozen chorus members. Nonspeaking extras may have helped fill the stage picture in occasional scenes such as Agamemnon's homecoming; but still, this expanse seems constructed for a larger, more spectacular form of entertainment. If this is true, then tragedy was an afterthought, and actors had to make do with physical surroundings they had inherited rather than originated.

THE DITHYRAMB

Although any event involving a substantial number of participants might have found a suitable home in a large orchestra, the dithyrambic contest is the most obvious and probable original occupant of the Greek theatre. These annual competitions involved twenty choruses composed of fifty members each, plus musician(s). Such a large group, dressed in elaborate costumes (Demosthenes provided golden crowns for his entry), would have produced an eye-filling spectacle that filled a large expanse such as the orchestra presented.

Evidence suggests that the earliest dithyrambs were brought to Corinth from Asia Minor around 600 BCE. Chronology muddies the case for the dithyramb as the original occupant of the theatre, since standard dating places the beginning of the Athenian dithyrambic contest some twenty-five years *after* the inauguration of tragic competition in 534 BCE. Dates for both dithyrambic and tragic contests are currently being questioned, but even if correct, they would not preclude the possibility that dithyrambic presentation began in Athens sometime *before* the competitions were established.

The standard textbooks confidently assert that the first tragic competitions at the City Dionysia took place in 534 BC and included plays by the tragedian Thespis, that dithyrambs were added in 508 BC, and that comedies followed in 486 BC. This scenario has been repeated so often that it has become one of the few fixed points in the otherwise shifting sands of fragmentary evidence, legend, and hypothesis that constitute what we know of early tragic performances. Based on a probable misreading of an inscription on a marble slab called the Marmor Parium (found on the Greek island of Paros and shipped to London in AD 1627), the conclusion that the Great Dionysia was instituted in 534 BC by the tyrant Peisistratus hardly seems secure.[1]

John Winkler writes that "dithyrambic and comic choruses are much older than these particular festival arrangements, which simply give a new financial and competitive structure to old traditions."[2] Dithyrambs were not abandoned as plays gained popularity; Pickard-Cambridge points out that "performances of dithyrambs were continually held in many parts of Greece in the third and second centuries B.C., and even down to the third century A.D."[3]

Surprisingly little is known about dithyrambic performance, and there is a tendency to view these contests as curtain-raising events preceding the more important tragedies. However, evidence indicates that Athens' dithyrambic competitions were grim, serious affairs, involving cutthroat competition between the rival factions. Demosthenes, *choregos* for one of his tribe's entries in mid-fourth century, supplies a vivid picture of the lengths to which his opposition would go in pursuit of a victory:

> Meidias bribed the umpires and so robbed my tribe unfairly of the prize, since I in person was struck by him and insulted as perhaps no chorusmaster was ever insulted before. . . . The trouble that he caused by opposing the exemption of our chorus from military service, . . . I will pass over in silence. . . . The sacred apparel provided for use at a festival I regard as being sacred until after it has been used — and the golden crowns, which I ordered for the decoration of the chorus, he plotted to destroy, men of Athens, by a nocturnal raid on the premises of my goldsmith. . . . He actually corrupted the trainer of my chorus. . . . He bribed the crowned Archon himself; he banded the choristers against me; he bawled and threatened, standing beside the umpires as they took the oath. . . . He blocked the doors of the paraskenia.[4]

Evidence here is in short supply, but if these bitter protestations can be taken as representative, the dithyrambic competitions fueled even stronger emotions than those attending the awarding of prizes for the tragedies and comedies.

The large number of participants in this annual event provides further evidence of its civic importance; Athens' ten tribes each entered two fifty-member choruses (men's and boys'), making a total of one thousand performers who appeared in the theatre during each City Dionysia.[5] By comparison, the tragic contest required a total number of performers equal to a single dithyrambic entry: twelve to fifteen chorus plus three actors times three entries. (Musicians, a problematic figure, are excluded from both counts.)

A major competition involves procedures and regulations which would tend to stabilize the physical surroundings. Demosthenes gives an example of this rule-making: "The law requires the archon to allot the pipers to the chorus-producers," adding that "there was much heated discussion and mutual recrimination between the Archon and the overseers of the tribe."[6] It is not difficult to envision a whole range of such tightly drawn rules and rigidly enforced regulations. Proof of tribal membership for each chorus member, for example, was vital: Andokides (the authorship is doubtful) writes that "the law allows anyone who wishes to expel any of the competing choral dancers who is a foreigner" and that Alkibiades, as a *choregos*, "drove him [a foreign boy] out with his fists."[7] With such a large and restive audience, some time restriction was surely in place; subject matter may have been kept within certain boundaries; costume style may have been specified, although to judge from Demosthenes' "golden crowns," expense was not a factor; perhaps there was a standard procedure governing entrances and exits of the choruses.

THE THEATRE AS DITHYRAMBIC PERFORMANCE SPACE

Did a structure evolve for staging the dithyramb *before* the birth of tragedy? The following sections examine the evidence concerning the various elements of the performance area to determine whether it better served the purposes of the dithyramb than those of tragedy.

The dithyramb has been, from the time of Aristotle, regarded as a possible precursor of tragedy. Fortunately for the present discussion, the seemingly endless origin-of-tragedy arguments need not concern us here, since there is no necessary connection between a space's original use and any subsequent applications: during the nineteenth century, for example, many acting troupes in the United States used courtrooms for theatres, but no one would argue that American drama had its origin in judicial proceedings.

The Orchestra

This 70-foot-wide space would be difficult to fill with the twelve to fifteen members of a tragic chorus. However, the fifty-member dithyrambic chorus could make effective use of this expanse in the presentation of the spectacle — whatever that may have been. The term "orchestra" (dancing place) is usually thought of as making a statement about the choreographic nature of the tragic chorus; but if the theatre existed before the birth of

FIGURE 30. *Euripides:* Stheneboia *(?): Würzburg. Courtesy of the Martin von Wagner-Museum der Universität Würzburg.*

tragedy, the term "dancing place" would initially have described its use for the dithyramb, not tragedy.

Paraskenia

Two south Italian vases from the fourth century BCE are the only existing representations of complete *skenai*. Both show clearly the *paraskenia* (literally, "beside-the-*skene*" structures). Both are kraters (large vessels for the mixing of wine and water), and both picture wooden *skenai*, as can be deduced from the thin columns supporting beams that span greater distances than would be possible with stone. The often-reproduced Würzburg fragment of a Tarentine calyx krater (fig. 30) shows the first meeting of Pelias and Jason; the two actors are placed in the area between the projecting *paraskenia*, while minor characters peep in at the doors (see the Bulle reconstruction, fig. 31). The other krater, now in the Louvre (fig. 32), shows a scene from *Iphigenia in Tauris*, with Iphigenia at one *paraskenion* and the statue of Artemis at the other; Orestes and Pylades occupy the space between. Neither of these paintings depicts a very effective scene design; bilateral symmetry and lack of center focus make for awkward dramatic

FIGURE 31. *The Bulle reconstruction. From Heinrich Bulle,* Eine Skenographie.

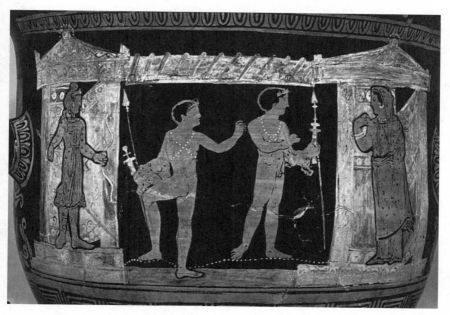

FIGURE 32. *Euripides,* Iphigenia in Tauris: *the Louvre, Paris. Courtesy of the Louvre, Paris.*

picturizations, a not infrequent condition in a less-than-ideal situation resulting from the use of found space.

Because these two vases do not support the standard views of the Greek *skene*, their validity has been questioned. Pickard-Cambridge rejects their testimony, stating that south Italian theatres "have little to contribute to our knowledge of the Athenian theatre, in which structures of a heavier type are implied by the massive foundations and other remains."[8] The wooden buildings shown on these vases obviously do not equate well with the "massive foundations" of Athens' later theatres, but Sir Arthur ignores the fact that Aeschylus, Sophocles, and Euripides wrote for the wooden *skenai* of fifth-century Athens, not the monumental stone versions of Hellenistic times. As late as mid-fourth century, Xenophon could rely upon his readers' acquaintance with wooden theatres in describing Cyrus' siege towers as resting upon "timbers as thick as those of the tragic stage."[9]

Further, it can be argued that evidence found outside Athens is quite capable of shedding light on Athenian theatre buildings; after all, play producers in the colonies of Magna Graecia were drinking from the same dramatic font as the playwrights and producers of Athens. There was considerable commerce, both material and intellectual, between southern Italy and the mother country. Aeschylus, it should be remembered, died on his *second* visit to Sicily. The *Iphigenia in Tauris* depicted on the Campanian krater may or may not be the Euripidean version, but it is at least a first cousin, definitely related in subject matter and probably possessing similar staging requirements. Oliver Taplin believes that acting troupes from Athens may have also made the journey: "If there were touring troupes within Attica, then, given the interest in Macedon, Sicily, etc., it is more than likely that sooner or later they extended their activities overseas."[10]

The Würzberg fragment and the Louvre krater constitute the only visual evidence of the complete *skene*. They cannot be dismissed as mere local eccentricities, particularly in the absence of firm evidence, either archaeological or written, contradicting their testimony.

But what purpose is served by this seemingly awkward arrangement of double doors set in DR and DL positions? One of Demosthenes' charges against his dithyrambic rival suggests a possible reason: "He [Meidias] blocked the paraskenia."[11] Apparently, the orator/*choregos* had planned to have his chorus enter (and perhaps exit) from one or both of the *paraskenia*; because he does not mention this use of the *paraskenia* as a special circumstance, one can surmise that they were the preferred — and perhaps even the prescribed — entrances for the contesting choruses.

A possible explanation for the existence of the *paraskenia* is supplied indirectly by W. M. Calder, a philologist concerned with the etymology of the word "dithyramb." Ordinarily, the term is thought to derive from the "twice-born" origin of Dionysos, who emerged first from his mother Semele and then again from the thigh of Zeus, where he was hidden to escape Hera's wrath upon finding evidence of her husband's philandering. Calder, however, traces the origin to a Phrygian word meaning "a tomb with double doors."[12] Although Calder made no such connection, he has here provided a description of the *paraskenion*.

Calder is concerned mainly with tombstones picturing a double door, "doorstones," as he calls them. He writes that "the 'double door' may refer to either a doorstone with two valves [that is, a tombstone picturing a double door], or to any doorstone as symbolically leading in two directions — outwards to the world of life, inwards to the world of death."[13]

> The religion of Phrygia, as Ramsay and others have shown by overwhelming evidence, centered in the cult of the grave. The family tomb (*progonikon* or *syggenikon*) [the Greek is here transliterated] was the *oikos* in which the dead lived, and a cardinal feature in sepulchral architecture was the door, occasionally called *thyra* on the monument, which provided communication between the living and the dead. . . . For the first element of *dithyrambos* the meaning of "grave" is attested. Comparing *dithyr-ambos* with *thri-ambos* and *iambos* we cannot doubt that the second element means "song" or a ritual performance of some kind, and we get the meaning of "grave-song" or "dirge" for the dithyramb.[14]

In the painted vases, as discussed in chapter 2, tomb entrances and *paraskenia/naiskoi* remained almost indistinguishable one from the other well into the fourth century. If the *paraskenia* had their origins in tomb entrances, then the emergence of the chorus from the *paraskenia*/tomb would fit the standard coming-of-spring resurrection theme that was essential to Dionysian ritual. There is no element of dirge in what little we know of Athenian dithyrambs; but as Calder writes, "In its passage from Asia to Greece the dithyramb, like Dionysos himself, changed its character."[15]

The entrance of the dithyrambic chorus through one or both of the *paraskenia* could well have been a prescribed part of the competition; symbolically, boys and young men would emerge from the grave, signaling the earth's rebirth in the spring of the year. If this scenario is correct, it is not difficult to understand why Demosthenes was upset at finding the doors blocked, forcing his group to enter through *parodoi* normally used for entrances of the tragic choruses. The *paraskenia* entrances were obviously significant; why else would Meidias have thought blocking them a worthwhile piece of skulduggery?

The "Royal" Door

Neither the Würzberg nor the Louvre krater has a center door. Was the door simply omitted by the painters to improve the composition? This seems unlikely; if a center door had existed, the dramatic composition would have focused around it.

Such a glaring deviation from received standard truth has usually been ignored or discounted, much as the testimony of the de Witt sketch showing the Swan theatre is routinely rejected because its arrangements do not square with accepted views of the Shakespearean theatre. Pickard-Cambridge, in the case of these kraters, predictably espouses the orthodox opinion; while calling the absence of center doors in the paintings "noteworthy," he dismisses the kraters as regional anomalies which "cannot be used to prove anything as regards the theatre of Dionysus at Athens."[16]

Sir Arthur is not alone in his rejection of these vases; scholarly affirmation of the UC door is nearly universal. Taplin states the commonly held opinion: "From *Oresteia* onward almost every tragedy makes use of a door in the skene as a means of entry and exit. . . . The door was presumably central, and must have been quite large, large enough for the operation of the ekkyklema."[17] Taplin's "presumably" is a more hedged declaration than most would make; T. B. L. Webster writes that "it is not however clear that any door except the central door was needed for fifth-century tragedy."[18] Audrey Stanley is particularly emphatic on the subject:

> The presentation of the *Oresteia* in 458 B.C. can scarcely be overemphasized in importance within the history of theatre architecture. All three plays demand a building with a central entrance: Agamemnon's palace in the first two plays, and two temples in the *Eumenides*. This innovative feature was obviously so needed by the drama that, with the exception of *Oedipus at Colonus* and possibly *Rhesus*, every other play following the *Oresteia* used a similar structure with a central entrance, whether this was a military hut (called a tent), a palace, a farmhouse or a cave.[19]

The support offered for the existence of the center door is concentrated in three areas: the application of theatrical common sense, which proclaims this UC entrance an absolute necessity; the dicta of Vitruvius and Pollux; and doors and porchlike structures from fourth-century Magna Graecia vases which are routinely construed as being in the UC position. Actual theatre remains are not helpful; the few theatre foundations showing evidence of upstage doors have them hidden behind the columns of the *proskenion*. Epidauros, for example, has three upstage entrances, but they are rendered nearly invisible by a row of *proskenion* columns: these "doors" were intended for access behind the large columns, not as stage entrances and exits.

Common sense may err in this case, although many centuries of theatrical practice have established the nearly absolute necessity of an UC entrance; imagining a stage lacking such a feature is difficult. However, theatre has sometimes flourished with only side entrances: if the de Witt sketch is to be given credibility, the Swan theatre of Elizabethan times lacked an UC entrance, and the Restoration stage operated with only entrances DR and DL, while the center proscenium area was reserved for scenic display. And there is a more modern example of this: early in the twentieth century, the UC entrance vanished from many theatres because of the introduction of the sky cyclorama. This German invention, the *Kuppelhorizont*, enjoyed a substantial Continental vogue; in the United States, the tiny Provincetown theatre and the Goodman theatre of Chicago installed encompassing plaster domes, and the University of Iowa surrounded its stage with an enormous U-shaped cloth cyclorama which all but eliminated the possibility of upstage entrances and exits. Somehow, theatre survived this limitation.

In regard to written testimony, the words of the Roman architect and the Greek lexicographer are routinely invoked to confirm the presence of a center entrance. Vitruvius first labeled this entrance the "Royal Door,"[20] a name still applied; both he and Pollux hypothesized a total of *three* doors set into the front of the Greek scene house.[21] Pollux writes that "of the three doors of the stage building, the middle one is a palace or cave or distinguished house or entirely belongs to the protagonist of the drama, while the right-hand one is the lodging of the deuteragonist, and the left-hand one contains the lowest character or a remote temple or is uninhabited."[22]

Many early twentieth-century reconstructions of Greek *skenai* included three doors (plus the doors of the *paraskenia*) as a standard feature, but at present flanking doors in the main scene house have fallen from favor. In the absence of any corroboration, it seems reasonable to conclude that both Pollux and Vitruvius were extrapolating backward in time from the three-doored, *paraskenia*-less Roman theatre with which both were familiar. The present-day cafeteria approach to these writers allows evidence for the center door to be accepted while statements about the flanking doors are rejected.

Visual evidence called up to support the presence of the center door comes from south Italian vase paintings of roughly the same period and provenance as the Würzberg and Louvre kraters. These typically show dramatic groupings around and beneath a roof supported by four thin wooden columns — although six and even eight are sometimes found. A set of double doors is pictured behind the "porch" in many of these vases; in others, doors are not shown, perhaps because they cluttered the painter's composition. Labeled *prothyron*, porch, *vestibulum*, *aedicula* — and the

FIGURE 33. *Euripides,* Andromache: *Milan. Courtesy of the Torno Collection, Milan.*

now fashionable *naiskos* — this flimsy structure is thought of as a kind of pavilion sitting in front of double doors in the Up Center position. Some writers visualize it as a permanent part of the *skene*, while others posit a portable structure, perhaps (if improbably) riding in on the *ekkyklema*.

Neglected in these interpretations is the obvious fact that the *naiskoi* are nearly identical to the *paraskenia* pictured in the Würzberg and the Louvre vases. (Seventeen examples are pictured in A. D. Trendall and T. B. L. Webster,[23] and many, many more have appeared since that volume was published in 1971.) An important but overlooked fact is that they sometimes show a continuing structure extending on only *one* side of the *naiskos* (figs. 33 and 34); not one shows walls (often indicated by columns) extending on both sides of the *naiskos*, as would be true if the structure were set

FIGURE 34. *Euripides,* Iphigenia in Tauris: *Naples. Photo courtesy of the Soprintendenza alle Antichità, Naples.*

in the middle of a building. These paintings are more likely to be views of a single *paraskenion* and part of the connecting building; the vase painters have chosen to represent only that side of the stage where dramatic action is taking place.

Confirmation of this interpretation is offered by a side-angled presentation of nearly all these paintings, as would be true if scenes were located in a SR or SL position. One exception, however (fig. 35), portrays the *naiskos* head-on; if all these pictures showed an UC porch, this balanced view would be the preferred compositional pattern for most painters, and one might expect to find more vases like this, rather than the lop-sided structures shown in figures 33 and 34. However, figure 35 does show, by its use of single-point perspective, that the more typical angled views do not result from the painters' inability to draw head-on.

Interpreting these paintings as a single *paraskenion* in a DR or DL position has the virtue of bringing the *naiskoi* representations into agreement with the Würzburg and Louvre kraters; they no longer need to be dismissed

FIGURE 35. *Euripides,* Iphigenia in Tauris: *St. Petersburg. Courtesy of the Hermitage Museum, St. Petersburg.*

as south Italian eccentricities. Rather, they are tributary theatres modeled after ones found in their mother country.

Interpreting the Comic Vases

The vase painters approach comic scenes differently from those of tragedy. The tragic *naiskos* scenes are generalized and idealized: porches, columns, and doors are remarkably similar throughout most of the vases. The putative actors are neither masked nor attired in stage costumes and appear to be of both sexes. Characters from several scenes are often combined in the painting. On the other hand, comic paintings are particularized, filled with realistic detail: actors wear masks of specific types; costumes show wrinkles and padding; scenes depict a particular stage moment rather than a general evocation of the entire play; the stage, where shown, appears to be a particular theatre in contrast to the generalized *naiskoi* structures.

For many years, these bawdy, low-comedy paintings were classified as *phlyakes,* regional entertainments only vaguely related to Athenian Old or

Middle Comedy. In recent times, scholars increasingly regard these *phylakes* as illustrations of mainstream Athenian comedy; Csapo and Slater, for example, argue convincingly that one vase shows a scene from Aristophanes' *Thesmophoriazusae*.[24]

It is difficult to reconcile the specific and often crudely constructed comic stages with the formal, idealized arrangement found in the tragic scenes. The tragic paintings, for example, show downstage columns blocking sight lines, but the comedy vases sight-line problems are solved by supporting the overhanging roof with angled braces tied to the door frame.[25]

The large doors with two shutters shown on the comic stage resemble the doors of tragedy in ornamental detail. When shown, comedy doors are usually in an Up Stage Right (USR) position, although occasionally they appear Up Stage Left (USL); apparently, painters felt free to represent only those architectural elements needed for storytelling and composition. Given the Greek fondness for symmetry, most of these comic stages probably had doors both R and L, although painters likely avoided cluttering their composition by eliminating either one set of doors or the other. Significantly, none of these paintings shows a center-positioned door, lending support to the preceding argument regarding the absence of a center door in the *skene*.

The Proskenion

The Würzburg and Louvre paintings both include an unadorned wall connecting the *paraskenia*; there is no indication of an upstage row of columns, a *proskenion*. The row of antefixes on the Würzburg fragment indicates the edge of a sloping tile roof that would require a supporting wall; Bulle's plan (fig. 36) conjectures a peaked roof. The krater at the Louvre shows a near-identical arrangement: "The two [sets of] doors are connected by a tiled roof, above what looks like a dark wall."[26]

Such architecturally uninteresting prospects cry out for ornamentation. William Bell Dinsmoor argues cogently that the original *proskenion* was a removable wooden structure put up in front of the *skene*. He cites a passage from Athenaeus (123:587b) which likens the *proskenion* to the courtesan Nannion:

> The comparison . . . suggests that in the minds of her contemporaries, the 'proscenium' was something that could easily be stripped away, leaving only bald nakedness. It was hardly a permanent architectural colonnade. It may have been some such temporary screen that caused Suidas to define proscenium as a 'curtain' before the scene building. . . . The

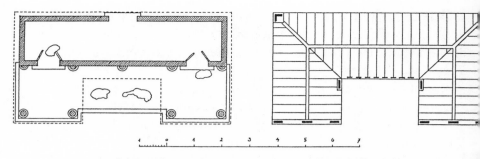

FIGURE 36. *Bulle's Würzburg roof reconstruction. From Heinrich Bulle,* Eine Skenographie.

FIGURE 37. *Sophocles,* Oedipus Tyrannos: *Syracuse. Courtesy of the Soprintendenza alle Antichità, Sicily.*

removable wooden proscenium was probably retained in Athens until about 150 BC.[27]

As *skenai* changed to stone construction, additional vertical roof supports may have been needed. The result was a colonnade which sat in front of the unadorned stage wall. The Oedipus vase (fig. 37), showing wooden columns, may picture the *proskenion* in an early stage of development.[28]

FIGURE 38. *Aphrodisias.*

While these columns served an aesthetic rather than dramatic function, they could be adapted to scenic purposes by fitting painted panels (*pinakes*) between them. Stone columns at Isthmia, Oropos, Priene, and Aphrodisias show cuttings for the insertion of these "flats" (fig. 38). Large, closely spaced, stone columns would, of course, have totally negated any possible dramatic use of doors standing further upstage.

However, the advent of the *proskenion* would have permitted the future birth of an Up Center door: circular holes in the floor and lintel, as at Oropos (fig. 39) and Isthmia, were undoubtedly intended to accommodate hinge pins for swinging panels or doors. In other words, the ancestral Royal Door was first inserted between two columns of the *proskenion*: when this center door was first introduced is problematic, but it was no earlier than the fourth century BCE, long after the surviving comedies and tragedies were first presented.

CONCLUSION

In order to reach any conclusion not cloaked in equivocation, some of the available evidence relating to the *skene* must be rejected, while other evidence is given prominence. For this discussion, the painters of the Würz-

FIGURE 39. *Oropos.*

burg and Louvre kraters are assumed to have provided a reasonably accurate picture of what they saw in the theatre. I have chosen to discount the testimony of Vitruvius and Pollux. Their writings are often unclear or ambiguous; they exhibit no particular affinity for the theatre and are clearly more influenced by the Roman theatre than the Greek. Moreover, of all the evidence available, these two writers are at the furthest chronological distance from the actual events.

For many centuries the dithyrambic contests maintained a primacy in the theatre. Because Athens was a democracy, political leaders would have responded more readily to the wishes of a thousand citizen/participants and their tribal supporters than to those of a few playwrights and a handful of actors. The performance needs of the dithyrambists must have been of primary importance in planning the theatre building. Even if actors and playwrights sought such innovations as an UC door, contest rules and the stabilizing effect of organized religion would have retarded the implementation of such an addition. However, a row of ornamental columns could have been added without affecting the basic dithyrambic performance schema.

Tragedy was born in found space created for the dithyramb. If this basic hypothesis is granted, the changes occurring in the *skene*'s configuration over two centuries proceed in a logical and orderly fashion. The likely course of this progression would begin with DR and DL *paraskenia* connected by a blank-fronted building; an ornamental colonnade (*proskenion*) was then added to relieve the severity of the unadorned center wall — at which point some scenic artist, chafing at his limited opportunities for expression, thought to insert painted flats (*pinakes*) between the columns. Finally, a further innovator placed a door between two of the upstage columns, marking the beginning of what culminated in the Roman theatre's Royal Door.

NOTES

1. Rush Rehm, *Greek Tragic Theatre*, 14–15. Csapo and Slater state that the Parian Stone was not inscribed until 264–263 BCE and that the "men's chorus" of 508 BCE (the traditional date for the beginning of dithyrambic competition) is only inferred to be a dithyrambic chorus (*The Context of Ancient Drama*, 120).

2. John J. Winkler, "The Ephebes' Song," in *Nothing to Do with Dionysos?* 203. The padded comic dancers of the *komast* vases date back to the seventh century.

3. A. W. Pickard-Cambridge, *The Dramatic Festivals of Athens*, 74.

4. Demosthenes, *Against Meidias*, 16–18.

5. Pickard-Cambridge, Bieber, and Rehm all say that only five men's and five boys' choruses competed each year in the City Dionysia, but evidence presented by Csapo and Slater indicates that each tribe entered both a men's and a boys' chorus annually. See *The Context of Ancient Drama*, 115–117.

6. Demosthenes, *Against Meidias*, 13–14.

7. Andocides, *Against Alkibiades*, 20. This is not an authentic oration, but rather "a literary exercise, perhaps composed during the fourth century but possibly later, drawing on an unknown source" (*Greek Orators IV: Andocides*, ed. and trans. Michael Edwards, 136).

8. A. W. Pickard-Cambridge, *The Theatre of Dionysus in Athens*, 172.

9. Xenophon, *Cyropaedia*, 6.1.54.

10. Oliver Taplin, *Comic Angels*, 91.

11. Later scholia frequently append *paraskenia* to ancient manuscripts, but Demosthenes' use of the term is the earliest known.

12. W. M. Calder, "The Dithyramb — An Anatolian Dirge," *Classical Review* 36 (1922): 13.

13. Ibid., 14. A double doorstone is pictured in W. M. Ramsay, *The Cities and Bishoprics of Phrygia*, 628.

14. Ibid., 13–14.

15. Ibid.

16. Pickard-Cambridge, *The Theatre of Dionysus in Athens*, 170.

17. Oliver Taplin, *The Stagecraft of Aeschylus*, 439.

18. T. B. L. Webster, *Greek Theatre Production* (1956 ed.), 10.

19. Audrey Stanley, "Early Theatre Structures in Ancient Greece: A Survey of Archaeological and Literary Records from the Minoan Period to 388 B.C.," 339.

20. Vitruvius, *De Architectura*, 5.6.3. The presence of a center door in the Greek theatre is never stated, but rather inferred from his general description of theatres both Greek and Roman.

21. Ibid., 5.6.8; Pollux, *Onomasticon*, 4.124.

22. Pollux, *Onomasticon*, 4.124–125.

23. See A. D. Trendall and T. B. L. Webster, *Illustrations of Greek Drama*, 94 (figs. III. 1,10; 1,17; 1,23; 2,8; 3,5; 3,9; 3,26; 3,27; 3,28; 3,29; 3,30(a); 3,30(b); 3,31; 3,32; 3,40; 3,43; 4,2).

24. Csapo and Slater, *The Context of Ancient Drama*, 67–69.

25. See Taplin, *Comic Angels*, 12:6 and 15:13. Alan Hughes shows an ornate roof supported by an angled swan's neck anchored to an upstage column ("Comic Stages in Magna Graecia," *Theatre Research International* 21 [1996]: plate 4).

26. Taplin, *Comic Angels*, 94.

27. William Bell Dinsmoor, *The Architecture of Ancient Greece*, 298–299.

28. If this row of columns were moved downstage some six or eight feet, it might have been covered by a flat porchlike projection, giving rise to the upper acting area of the Hellenistic period.

6

STAGE MACHINERY

A mountain of speculation has centered upon the mechanical devices the Greeks used to enhance performances of their plays. Many versions of these devices have been proposed, ranging from simplistic to overengineered.

THE *MECHANE*

Use of the *mechane* is not spelled out in the tragic scripts, although Taplin speculates on its appearance as early as *Prometheus Bound*.[1] The metaphoric image of a machine-transported god who appears in the midst of a tragic muddle is first found in Plato around 384 BCE;[2] about the same time, Demosthenes speaks of Timocrates appearing "like a god from the machine."[3] This usage as a standard figure of speech indicates that the *mechane* was well known to the Athenians. Though it may have found wide application in the tragedies, the *mechane*'s existence is mainly documented by Aristophanes in his comedies. In *The Peace*, Trygaeus' flight on a gigantic dung beetle is surely a caricature of some character from tragedy flying about on a horse, bull, dragon, or other creature. Socrates, in *The Clouds*, first appears suspended above the other actors and later descends to the stage. Assuming the possibility of more than one *mechane*, the feathered creatures in *The Birds* may all have flown about the orchestra, and surely Iris, goddess of the rainbow, would also have had the gift of flight. In *Thesmophoriazusae*, Euripides flies on in the wing-footed guise of Perseus. In *The Acharnians*, the costume of Bellerophon is discussed, offering the possibility that Euripides' crippled hero from the lost *Sthenoboia* may have traveled across the stage on a winged Pegasus.

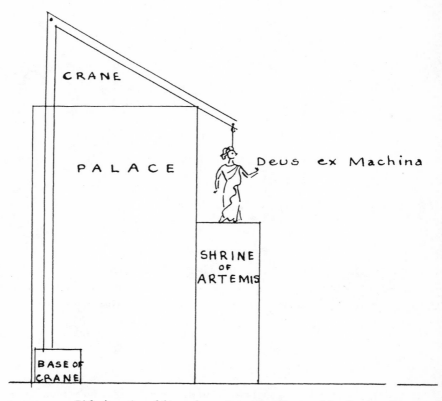

FIGURE 40. *Bieber's version of the* mechane. *From* The History of the Greek and Roman Theatre, *copyright Princeton University Press, 1939, 1961; renewed 1989 by Princeton University Press.*

Ropes and rigging were undoubtedly used in the operation of this device. Much later, in the eighteenth century, sailors worked the complicated rope-and-pulley scene-shifting machines of Sweden's Drottningholm theatre; perhaps the Greeks, in similar fashion, relied upon nautical expertise to help solve their flying problems.

Many scholars have tried their hands at re-creations of this machine. Margarete Bieber's unworkable *mechane* (fig. 40) is an example of the fanciful and impractical; even with the advantages of structural steel and electric welding, such a device would be nearly impossible to construct and operate. Even if it could be built, the *deus* (or comedy figure) would be limited to takeoff and landing only from the radius of the arm's rotation.

Heinrich Bulle and Heinrich Wirsing (fig. 41) approach the problem in markedly different fashion — although their creation also restricts possible stage positions to the arc of its rotating arm. Radically different from

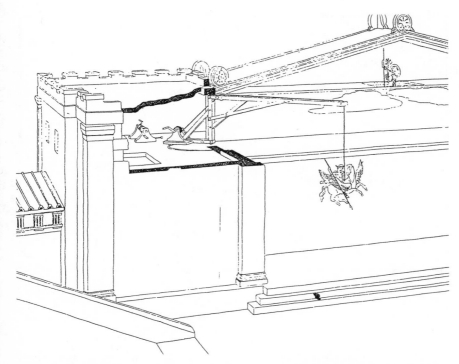

FIGURE 41. *The Bulle-Wirsing version of the* mechane. *From Heinrich Bulle and Heinrich Wirsing,* Szenebilder zum Griechischen Theatre des 5. Jahrhunderts v. Chr.

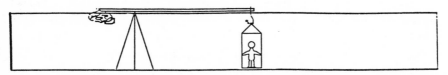

FIGURE 42. *Mastronarde's version of the* mechane. *From Donald J. Mastronarde, "Actors on High," 293, copyright by the Regents of the University of California: reprinted from* Classical Antiquity *9 (October 1990).*

Bieber's fanciful design, the version of these Germans is a ponderous piece of construction equipment more appropriate for hoisting marble blocks into place on temple walls. While the small drum of the windlass can hoist very heavy loads, a stage eternity would be needed to crank the mounted figure up or down — assuming that Bellerophon could somehow maintain his seat on a gravely out-of-balance Pegasus.

Donald J. Mastronarde's version requires a "trapeze" hung from the end of a long pole; the actor stands on the bar until he dismounts, either in the orchestra or on the roof (fig. 42). As in the previous two re-creations, the

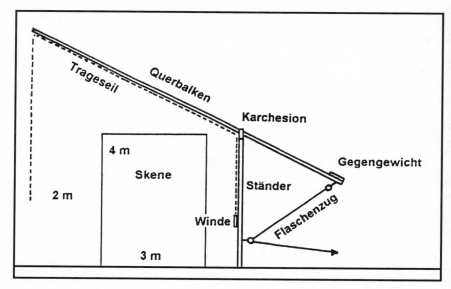

FIGURE 43. *Lendle's version of the* mechane. *From Egert Pöhlmann,* Studien zur Bühnendichtung und zum Theaterbau der Antike, *copyright Professor Dr. Egert Pöhlmann.*

actor's position would be restricted to the radius of the pole's movement. Also, the actor's physical expressiveness would be restricted, since he must keep a grip on the supporting ropes.[4]

Otto Lendle most recently examined the problems of reconstructing the crane.[5] After looking at two rather dubious possibilities, the *Einmastkran* and the *Schiffskran*, he settled on the *Hebemaschine*, a long, counterweighted pole. His "mast," perhaps unworkably long at 13 m (43 feet), is controlled from behind a flat-roofed scene house, which provides masking for the machine's operators (fig. 43). To allow movement of the mast, Lendle makes use of a device mentioned by Vitruvius and Polybius, the *karchesion*. As plausibly reconstructed by J. G. Landels,[6] this swiveling mechanism would permit easy and rapid movement of the long mast. The name apparently derives from a resemblance to either the Greek *karxesion*, "a goblet narrower in the middle than at top or bottom," or the Roman *carchesium*, "an oblong beaker with handles." Its exact form, and whether the *karchesion* was in use more than three centuries before Vitruvius' writings, remains unknown.

Unlike the other versions, Lendle provides a raise-and-lower line attached to the *deus* figure; this line, combined with an accompanying raising or lowering of the beam, makes it possible to place an actor anywhere within the arc commanded by the machine. However, neither Lendle nor

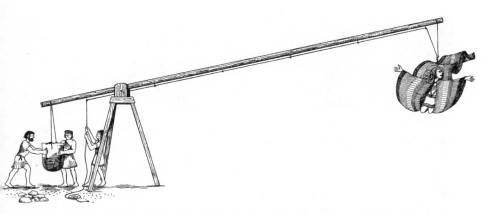

FIGURE 44. *Iris flying from Ashby's version of the* mechane. *Artist's conception by Elaine Atkinson.*

any of the other reconstructors has considered that a single rope would allow its load to revolve uncontrollably. In the Italian Renaissance, technicians sometimes used single lines to suspend gilded *putti* that floated about the heavens; but even with the advantage of tightly woven brass ropes, they used two points of suspension when a figure's orientation was to be maintained. Not long ago, I watched the Ghost of Marley clutch frantically at a chimney pot over Scrooge's bedroom as he struggled to face his audience; he was suspended from a single cable.

Mastronarde feels that "scholars seem to be embarrassed by what they regard as the absurdity and clumsiness of the device and . . . worry whether an entrance on the crane might reduce the dignity of tragedy."[7] Viewed from our technologically advanced age, the Greek *mechane* must have looked pretty silly: an actor suspended in broad daylight from some sort of wooden arm — without the present-day advantages of thin steel cables, masking flats, draperies, and controllable lighting. The absurdity of the situation calls to mind Ben Jonson's assessment of the Elizabethan *mechane*: The "creaking throne comes down the boys to please."[8] The Elizabethan playwright's sensibilities may have been offended by such a primitive device, but nevertheless the throne did come down and it did please — at least the more spectacle-seeking portion of the audience, which surely included some adults as well as London apprentices stealing an afternoon away from their duties.

Most reconstructions pay little attention to the protocols of scene-shifting, which require that changes be made smoothly and without apparent effort. Above all, the shift should be performed with the utmost dispatch. The version I have devised conforms to these requirements (fig. 44).

FIGURE 45. *Lodgepole pines for the* mechane *reconstruction.*

A slender 40-foot-long pole rests on a fulcrum 8 feet from the butt end, which is counterweighted to compensate for the mechanical advantage of the person suspended from the onstage end of the pole; 600 pounds of sand, rocks, slag (from Athens' forges), or even lead from the mines at nearby Laurion and Thorikos would balance a 150-pound actor — plus some additional weight for the pole itself. The actor and his balancing load need not be exactly equal if two husky stagehands are available to pull up or push down on the counterweight as needed.

To maintain orientation, a double-purchase pulley arrangement would be the simplest and easiest method; this would avoid the spinning-actor problem while still keeping control from a single line; the operator handling the rope, given a two-to-one mechanical advantage, would also find his task made lighter. By raising or lowering the butt of the pole and simultaneously adjusting line length, an actor could land or fly off anywhere within a 32-foot radius. Although scenic items like a winged horse or a dung beetle would increase the counterweighting requirement, such a flight would still be within the realm of possibility; in these instances, a suspending harness of three or four ropes might be used. The fulcrum, a wooden or possibly stone pylon, would work most effectively if it were slightly taller than the *skene*; as a refinement, operators and counterweights might be concealed behind the peaked roof that Bülle visualizes for the Würzburg *skene*, lending at least a hint of stage magic to the necessarily clumsy proceedings.

Presently, plans are being completed to build an actual *mechane* capable of moving an actor about the stage. Several straight, slender, 40-foot Wyoming lodgepole pine trees have been cut and peeled (fig. 45); after the wood has dried and snows have melted on Casper Mountain, a working model of the Greek *mechane* will be constructed. Professor W. P. Vann, of Texas Tech University's civil engineering department, has agreed to co-direct this project.

Ramps and the Unlikelihood of a Raised Stage on a Flat Roof

There are limits to primitive flight. The flaming chariot hypothesized (on very little evidence) for Medea's final departure, replete with fire-snorting dragons and recently expired children, would have been too heavy and cumbersome to permit flying. *If* such a conveyance was indeed used in the production, ramps to an upper level would have allowed a chariot with dragon-costumed horses to attain some elevation above the actor playing a distraught Jason. Conceivably, large, articulated puppet dragons could have been attached to a chariot that was pulled across the stage by a hidden rope;

FIGURE 46. *The ramp at Sikyon.*

this scheme would work for the *Medea* vase shown in Trendall and Webster (fig. III.3,34).

Theatrical ramps allow objects to be rolled from one level to another; however, they require more horizontal space than is needed by stairs to reach a given elevation. (Greek ramps and steps are both steeper than those of the present day.) As suggested in the previous chapter, this narrow raised stage probably sat in front of the *skene* and was supported by the columns of the *proskenion*. One stage ramp survives at Sikyon, because the builders found it easier to incorporate an outcropping of living rock into the design than to hack it away (fig. 46). Since no trace of rutting can be discerned in the Sikyon ramp, it may be that wheels and hooves were padded to enhance the illusion of flight.[9]

Ramps usually run between flat landings at both upper and lower terminations; this fact has reinforced the supposition that the scene house was built with a flat roof. Three reconstructions shown here (Bieber, Mastronarde, and Lendle) all assume that the *skene* had a flat roof, one which doubled as a performance area.

The roof-top stage has long been regarded as a *sine qua non* of Greek theatres, an absolute necessity for performance of the tragedies. However, no archaeological evidence verifies the existence of flat roofs in Greek architecture. (Flat roofs cause maintenance problems, as can be seen today in the lamentable condition of Frank Lloyd Wright's Fallingwater.) Innumerable digs at Greek sites have unearthed only public buildings with slanted tile roofs; vases from Magna Graecia show either a peaked tile roof or a row of antefixes marking the edge of a tile roof. These tiles were usually terra-cotta, but some buildings (such as the temple at Bassae) were roofed with cut-marble tiles.

Two scraps of information about scene house roofs are found in Aristophanes' *The Clouds* and *The Wasps*. In *The Wasps*, Philocleon is first heard rummaging around beneath the tiles of the roof: The script definitely says "tile" or collectively "tiling" (*keramis*, 206), which means that a raked rather than flat roof was present. In this comedy, Philocleon, seeking to escape from his house, climbs into the attic. The low pitch of Greek roofs allowed tiles to be held in place mainly by gravity, so Philocleon would have produced quite a clatter by pushing at them from below. In this case, the actor probably removed a tile and peered out at the audience, for Bdelycleon, standing below, remarks on being struck by a piece of falling dirt (203), undoubtedly some of the clay or plaster used for bedding the tiles. (Tiles measuring more than one meter square have been conjectured.)[10] In *The Clouds*, an exasperated Strepsiades sets fire to the *rafters* of the Thoughtery. (The word *dokos* [1496] can mean either "beam" or "rafter," but is usually translated as the latter.)[11]

Both references point strongly to the presence of a peaked tile roof on the scene house. If a level, raised performance area did exist in Classical times, as was true of the late Hellenistic theatre at Priene, it must have been a kind of porch supported by columns of the *proskenion*. There is no evidence that Classical Greeks covered their buildings with flat roofs.

There can be little doubt that a large, flat, upper-level acting area would have been useful in staging the tragedies, but usefulness does not necessarily result in actuality; the plays could have been performed with occasional actors treading a tiled, slanted roof. As discussed in the previous chapter, "found space" involves making-do. Greek roofs were not as steeply pitched as those found in rainy England; assuming a weight-bearing potential for the tiles (they have been found in varying thicknesses), an actor could negotiate such a surface without sliding off or crashing through.

Two examples will show how scenes might have been staged without a raised stage. In *Agamemnon*, the Watchman who provides the exposition may have stood either on the ridge pole or on the edge of the roof; since he has spent many years as a lookout, a little perch may have been built for him to pass the lonely hours of the night.

Five characters appear above the orchestra in Euripides' *Orestes*, creating a more substantial problem than that of the single Watchman. Orestes and Pylades (a mute) enter above, holding the hapless (and also mute) Hermione between them; the scene would be most dramatically effective if they stood at the very edge of the roof as Orestes threatens to cut Hermione's throat and hurl her to the ground below. Apollo's subsequent appearance as *deus ex* is easily accomplished by use of the *mechane* — but a further problem arises when Helen makes a ghostly visit. Flying two people simultaneously from one crane would be difficult, but since Helen is a nonspeaking ghost, she might have been represented only by her mask and some trailing draperies. Or she could have appeared on the ridge pole while Apollo hovered above. Another possibility is that she was flown in on a second *mechane*. The use of more than one flying machine has been little discussed, but several of these devices might have been used simultaneously, as suggested earlier for *The Birds*.

The Ekkyklema

Although the word *ekkyklema* was liberally added by later scholiasts to the margins of play manuscripts, the word is not found before the second century CE writings of Pollux. His account is both confused and confusing: "The ekkyklema is a high podium on beams, on which rests a throne; it looks down on unspeakable deeds committed behind the skene in the houses. The thing on which the ekkyklema is introduced is called an eiskyklema. One must assume this for each door." [12]

The *ekkyklema* has received a variety of mind's-eye visualizations. Some see it as a revolving stage with a masking screen in the middle, which somehow must be able to work in conjunction with a set of double doors. Webster, one of the more production-oriented classicists, posits a twelve-foot opening, "the minimum desirable," [13] which necessitates a pair of ponderous six-foot doors to allow a rectangular stage wagon to roll forth. Aside from the difficulties of engineering a clear twelve-foot span, such large doors, whether swinging out or in, pose nearly insuperable difficulties.

Pickard-Cambridge must be commended for adopting the simplest and most practical solution to the problems posed by the *ekkyklema*. [14] For *The Acharnians*, rather than using a large stage wagon, he would have the actor playing Euripides "wheeled out" reclining upon a chaise; the ragged costumes of the Euripidean tragic heroes remain offstage, and a servant (as specified by the script) is sent to fetch the various items as they are needed. The dialogue does not imply an interior scene, but rather suggests that the

FIGURE 47. *Chaeremon:* Achilles. *Courtesy of the Museum of Fine Arts, Boston.*

playwright is brought forth from his dwelling. (Dikaeopolis' reference to "up there," while conceivably placing the *ekkyklema* on a second level, can also be translated "with your feet up," as on a chaise.)

In similar fashion Agathon, the cross-dressing playwright of the *Thesmophoriazusae*, could be trundled forth on a chaise. Modern productions would tend to make this scene a revealed interior, with Agathon's boudoir resembling a RuPaul vision of paradise; however, the scene could be staged in much simpler fashion if the few required properties were added to Agathon's chaise/wagon and rolled out as a unit.

Pickard-Cambridge's rolling chaise/*ekkyklema* would easily pass through *paraskenia* doors — or a central door of comparable size, assuming that one existed. Paintings (fig. 47) show roofed structures filled with properties that could easily be shifted on wheels: altars, thrones, couches, and statues are common.[15] In regard to fig. 4, chapter 2, Trendall and Webster speculate that "the appearance of Alkestis on the couch was probably brought about by the use of the *ekkyklema*; it would have been wheeled inside after her death."[16] (See also vase paintings in chapter 5.)

Display of the dead has long been regarded as a traditional bit of tragic stage business, probably springing from Pollux's statement that the *ekkyklema* "looks down on unspeakable deeds committed behind the *skene*" (132). Exhibiting the victims on a rolling stage is effective theatre, consonant with the apparent prohibition forbidding onstage acts of violence. Showing the presumably bloodied bodies of the slain would visually confirm the consequences of offstage deeds, also providing an effective stage picture. Rehm feels that such display is essential, going so far as to suggest that if the *ekkyklema* had not been invented when *Agamemnon* was first presented, "then servants carried out the bodies and dumped them on the ground, while Clytemnestra took up her position behind them."[17] Mortuary displays may be effective, but such a staging technique is not verifiable. Vases frequently show dead figures because their presence is necessary for the painter's telling of a story; offstage events frequently appear on theatrical vases. No tragic text, however, specifies a showing of bodies, nor is there any supporting evidence beyond the pronouncements of Pollux and the later marginalizers.

The Periaktoi

Theatre designers of the Italian Renaissance were fascinated by a scenic device found in the rediscovered manuscript of Vitruvius' *De Architectura*.

> These are called *periaktoi* in Greek from the three-sided machines which turn having on their three sides as many kinds of subject. When there are to be changes in the play or when the gods appear with sudden thunders, they are to turn and change the kind of subject presented to the audience. Next to these the angles of the walls run out which contain the entrances to the stage[,] one from the public square and the other from the country.[18]

Vitruvius' description does not spring from firsthand observation, since the device was not used in the Roman theatre. Nevertheless, these triangular devices (also mentioned by Pollux) provided an exercise in re-creation for Italian court designers. Because neither the size nor the shape of the triangle was specified in *De Architectura*, a considerable range of interpretations is possible. Beginning in mid-sixteenth century, platoons of triangles marched across Renaissance stages, some large and equilateral like those of Giacomo

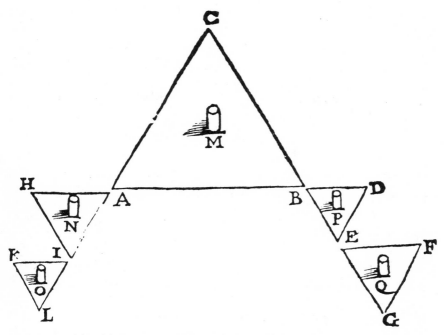

FIGURE 48. *Vignola's* periaktoi. *From* Le due regole della prospettiva pratica *(1583) by* Giacomo Barozzio da Vignola.

Barozzio da Vignola (fig. 48), others with smaller right triangles as diagrammed by Joseph Furttenbach (fig. 49). Some Renaissance *periaktoi* had as many as six sides.

No confirming evidence verifying the use of *periaktoi* has been uncovered. If these triangular objects did indeed have a Greek existence, one might expect a mention in earlier writings, or at least the unearthing of a painted vase showing something that might be construed as having a triangular shape. Based upon present knowledge, *periaktoi* should be regarded as either a misinterpretation of evidence by later writers or perhaps a folkloric legend. The *periaktoi* were not practical theatre devices; even during the Renaissance, they enjoyed only a brief vogue before being superseded by the pole-and-chariot method of scene shifting.

CONCLUSION

Historically, there have been times when technology overwhelmed the working theatre. Jean de La Fontaine found the French theatre of the seventeenth century hamstrung by an elaborate system of ropes and pulleys:

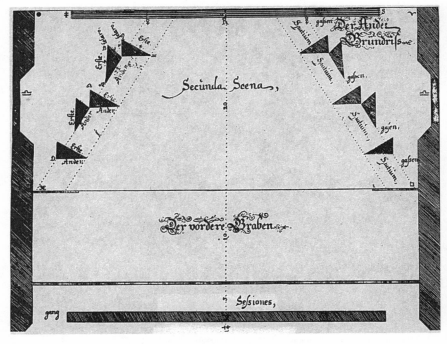

FIGURE 49. *Furttenbach's* periaktoi. *From* Architectura recreationis *(1640) by Joseph Furttenbach the Elder.*

> I never find, when the prompter signals, "Next,"
> Scenes change as fast as in the text.
> Counterweights stick; a god who intervenes
> Caught in mid-air cries out on the machines.
> A tuft of trees juts from the ocean's swell,
> And half of Heaven remains in the midst of Hell.

More recently, in mid-twentieth century, theatre was beset by complex, confusing, and supremely unreliable dimming systems, resulting in a period when many performances were lit spasmodically — and some not at all.

However, there is no evidence to indicate that Classic Greek theatre ever became a prisoner of the technician. Vase paintings show little variation in theatrical structures through the fourth century; if machinery had come to the forefront, some changes would be evident.

Given a slow speed of scenic innovation in Classical times, the limited technology available, the absence of masking curtains or flats, and the revelatory properties of daylight, the Greeks undoubtedly opted for the simplest and easiest solutions to their shifting problems. The *mechane* probably consisted of a counterweighted pole with a pulley-operated rope on the end. The *ekkyklema* would have been little more than a chaise-on-wheels; perhaps thrones, altars, and statues were also mounted on casters. There is no evidence supporting a flat-roofed *skene* in Classical times; the later raised stage of the *thyroma* theatre was a projecting porch, not a roof. Clambering around on slanted rooftops may not the most dignified of acting techniques, but actors adjust to found space. A lack of confirming evidence militates against the *periaktoi*, and its necessary size is also a problem: to be visible in such a large theatre, *periaktoi* must be minimally six feet on each panel, and their presence anywhere on the stage would impede the flow of traffic; a change in location could be spelled out more easily with *pinakes* placed in front of the blank upstage wall or in later theatres inserted between the *proskenion* columns.

As shown in the discussions of the previous chapter, the writings of Vitruvius and Pollux are too often provably wrong to be used as bases for scenic reconstructions. The demands of an outdoor situation and the absence of camouflage for technical contrivances make simple devices the more likely.

NOTES

1. Oliver Taplin, *The Stagecraft of Aeschylus* (Oxford: Oxford University Press, 1977), 250–262.

2. Plato, *Cratylus*, 425d. The tragic *mechane* is also employed metaphorically in *Clitopho*, 407A. Plato's authorship of the latter is not certain.

3. Demosthenes, *Against Boeotus*, 2.59.

4. Donald J. Mastronarde, "Actors on High: The Skene Roof, the Crane, and the Gods in Attic Drama," *Classical Antiquity* 9 (October 1990): 247–294.

5. Otto Lendle, "Überlegungen zum Bühnenkran," in Egert Pöhlmann, *Studien zur Bühnendichtung und zum Theaterbau der Antike*, 165–172.

6. J. G. Landels, *Engineering in the Ancient World* (Berkeley: University of California Press, 1978), 94–98.

7. Mastronarde, "Actors on High," 270–271.

8. Ben Jonson, prologue to *Every Man in His Humor*.

9. There is also evidence that ramps were present at the theatre of Epidauros. See Armin von Gerkan and Wolfgang Müller-Wiener, *Das Theater von Epidauros*, plate 14. Aldo Neppi Modona reports evidence of ramps at Oropos (figs. 27 and 28) and Corinth (figs. 36 and 37) in *Gli edifici teatrali greci e romani*.

10. A. Trevor Hodge, *The Woodwork of Greek Roofs*, 8.

11. A. Trevor Hodge writes that *dokos* "is the term usually applied to large timbers such as would be suitable for use as purlins [horizontal cross members of a roof] or ridge beam" (123).

12. Pollux, *Onomasticon*, 4.127–128. The word *ekkyklema* is thought to be related to *ekkyklein* and *eiskyklein*, verbs found in plays of Aristophanes where some sort of wheeled conveyance is required.

13. T. B. L. Webster, *Greek Theatre Production* (1956 ed.), 8–9.

14. A. W. Pickard-Cambridge, *The Theatre of Dionysus in Athens*, 100–122.

15. See A. D. Trendall and T. B. L. Webster, *Illustrations of Greek Drama*, figs. III. 1,10; 1,17; 3,5; 3,27; 3,29; 3,30a; 3,30b; 3,31; 3,32; 3,40; 4,2; 5,4.

16. Ibid., 75.

17. Rush Rehm, *Greek Tragic Theatre*, 156, n. 6.

18. Vitruvius, *De Architectura*, 5.6.8.

7

THE ORIENTATION
OF GREEK THEATRES

During the late nineteenth and early twentieth centuries, theories attempting to explain the orientation of buildings in ancient Greece received considerable scholarly attention. But even during the heyday of siting studies theatres were usually passed over, with attention focused on temples. Von Gerkan and Müller-Wiener gave theatre some passing attention, attempting to show a total nonrelevance of orientation to their placement; to demonstrate the randomness of siting, they included a selection of theatre bearings in their work on Epidauros (fig. 50).[1] Using only twenty-seven theatres from Greece and Anatolia, they had their audiences facing in all directions; in order to fill in a blank portion of their compass rose, these German archaeologists found it necessary to include the westward-facing but purely Roman theatre at Hierapolis — while ignoring the remains of a nearby Hellenistic theatre in which the audience looked almost due south.

In 1939, the respected William Bell Dinsmoor made an "attempt to revive orientation studies of Greek buildings." He tried to "illustrate a method of obtaining more accurate information concerning the dates of Greek temples and certain details of religious practice through the application of an outmoded theory, that of 'orientation.'"[2] When this complex study, replete with trigonometric calculations of seasonal star positions, met with little favor, orientation became a dead issue for several decades, only reviving briefly in 1962 with the publication of Vincent Scully's *The Earth, the Temple, and the Gods.*

Scully argues that many Greek public buildings were sited in terms of their relationship to visible topographic features; he finds that the most

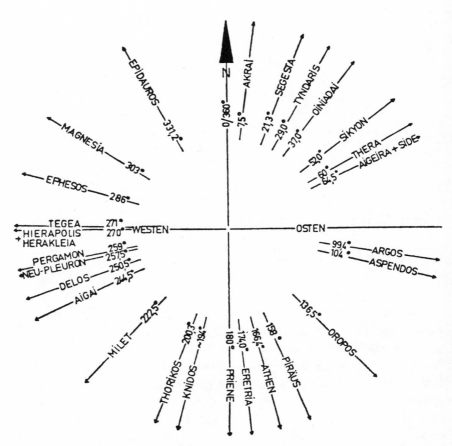

FIGURE 50. *Von Gerkan and Müller-Wiener's diagram of the theatre orientation. From*
Das Theatre von Epidauros.

notable landmarks are mountains or hills, which in his panoramic lexicon
became horns or breasts, and clefts, which became horns, breasts, or female
genitalia. Needless to say, the mountainous regions of Greece lend themselves to horns and breasts and clefts. On the siting of the theatre at Mega-
lopolis, he writes, "The theater, intended to accommodate the crowd at the
meetings of the [Arcadian] League and therefore overlarge itself, is oriented
directly toward the single high conical peak which marks the ridge line to
the north. Near the peak is a cleft in the ridge which *might perhaps* be *interpreted* as a *rather indefinite* pair of horns" (emphasis added).[3]

Though this work was popular enough to require two editions, the concepts found little resonance in the archaeological world. In the preface to
the later edition, Scully writes, "I am somewhat exasperated by recent publications of Greek sites. The landscape still does not exist so far as their

authors are concerned, despite obvious human identifications with land-scape in Greece and elsewhere throughout history. Such obdurate blindness now seems hardly less than humanistically irresponsible."[4]

In 1972, a dissertation dealing somewhat with orientation was completed in the School of Education at New York University. Written by Alwyn P. H. Scott, the work is titled "A Speculative Study to Search for the Genesis of the Architectural Form of the Ancient Greek Theatre to Indicate a Possible Origin of Greek Drama in Calendar-Fixing." Scott "attempts to describe formal similarities . . . between Megalithic calendar-fixing cromlechs [as found at Stonehenge] and the Theatre of Dionysus at Athens." He finds that "the *theatron* itself . . . may have evolved its shape and size originally from an archaic astronomical useage [*sic*]."[5]

THEORIES OF ORIENTATION

Aside from the hypotheses of Scott and Scully, there are two more pedes-trian considerations offered to explain the orientations of the theatres. The first states (or more often implies) that a particular hillside was chosen be-cause it offered the fewest construction problems and the most convenient access for audiences. The second, based upon visits to theatre sites by vari-ous authors, tends to partially agree with Scully in stating that the sites were chosen primarily for their view.

Random Orientation

The "random hillside" approach would ignore compass direction, sug-gesting that the builders sought only a suitably graded slope in an accessible location. If the hill is of rock, risers can be chiseled out; if of dirt, quarried stone can be brought in. Should this happen to be a traditional gathering place of the citizenry, so much the better.

Tradition involving the reuse of old sites certainly played a part in site selection, for we have evidence that many theatres, especially in Anatolia, were built in the same locations as older ones. But it is likely that the original choice of a particular site was based upon suitability; reuse would merely confirm this.

Theatres were, however, sometimes transferred to different locations. Athenians, after a presumably catastrophic bleacher collapse in the Agora, rebuilt their theatre on the south slope of the akropolis; the new theatre at Argos (099°) was cut into the same hill only a hundred yards distant from an earlier straight-rowed theatre (141°); Hierapolis built a new theatre for its new city, located a quarter mile from the old one.

The major drawback to the random hillside theory is that no attention is paid to the seasonal position of the sun, the Greeks' only source of heat and light for their theatres. The theory also fails to account for the use of inconvenient sites, such as the one at Chaironeia, where the difficulties encountered in constructing the later *theatron* must have been anticipated from work done on an earlier straight-rowed version. In spite of this, the Chaironeans persisted in carving out a new structure on this very steep hill of hard marble. Lacking a natural hollow, the seating on the sides of the orchestra required the importation of large quantities of fill dirt (now vanished) to complete the side seating of the *theatron*. The hillside portion of the *theatron* was pitched steeply enough to cause vertigo, and the theatre faced north, statistically the least popular direction. Was the location badly chosen? In a way it was: half-hearted chisel marks on the upper hillside section show where the builders started to remove the solid rock overburden to give a more gradual rake to the auditorium; instead they settled for a vertiginous rise and a fourth-balcony view of the stage. Situated in typical fashion on a slope outside the walls of the akropolis, the site could have been moved to a more easily worked hillside. Wrong-headedness may possibly explain the choice of this site, but construction suitability does not.

The View

The other suggestion offered for the choice of one hillside location over another is that the preferred site offers a prettier prospect. Scully, in addition to his advocacy of natural landmarks as a basis for site choice, believes that panorama was a primary consideration. He writes of "the role of the Greek theater in providing an architectural shape within which the earth's own hollows could be experienced and from which the farther landscape could be sympathetically viewed." He concludes that "the importance of the theater in creating sweeping views for Hellenistic cities can therefore not be overestimated." [6]

This reasoning extrapolates from our modern response to panoramas: each year, Californians by the thousands journey some fifty miles to the slopes of Mount Tamalpais to attend an afternoon performance of a Broadway musical set against a breathtaking view of San Francisco Bay. For people who spend most of their lives within the confines of four walls and a ceiling, this pilgrimage kindles a reawakening to the beauties of the outdoors. But would people who lived all of their days on the slopes of Mount Tamalpais find the view so inspiring? George Bean writes of this attempt to inflict our modern outlook upon the ancients:

> The view from the theatre at Teos has aroused the enthusiastic admiration of modern writers. It embraces the site of the city, the harbor, and the coast as far as the promontory of Myonnesus. "How intensely," says Hamilton, "the contemplation of such a scene must have heightened the enjoyment of the spectator during a performance of the *Agamemnon* or the *Medea*." Ximinez, in his *Asia Minor in Ruins*, goes even further: "In choosing the position of a theatre the Greeks' first thought was for the landscape they would have before them." This, in the present writer's opinion, is a misconception. . . . Performances in ancient theatres were special occasions, confined to a limited number of days in a year; the spectators assembled to watch a play, and it is unlikely they gave a thought to scenery familiar to them all their lives. Indeed, it is doubtful if a view of this kind would have impressed them much. Sea and shore, mountains and blue skies are commonplace in Greek lands; we think them beautiful, but the Greeks preferred a good well-watered arable plainland. The writer once commented to a peasant in Attica on the beauty of the scenery; he smiled at my quaint foreign enthusiasm and replied: "Too many stones."[7]

It should also be noted that many theatre builders did not choose particularly inspiring views. At Kassope, a thoroughly planned Hellenistic instant city, the theatre was built facing inward toward the civic center rather than upon the adjacent hillside, which commands a breathtaking view of the ocean and coastline. Scully, confronted by this viewless theatre, concluded that "the town as a whole is shaped like a theater . . . [and] a mighty panorama opens out before it."[8]

Consider, too, that our present enjoyment of these vistas is unobstructed by scene houses that would have blocked the view for those ancients seated below the *diazoma*. Should the plays have proven dull in ancient times, the priests and city fathers in the bottom rows had only the scenic facade for diversion; they could not have passed the time in watching a flock of sheep grazing on the distant hillside or a ship beating to windward across the harbor. (Scully believes that the *skene* and *theatron* of the Greek theatre were purposely left unfused so that "the greater scale of the natural landscape could open out to left and right, or from the upper seats, above.")[9]

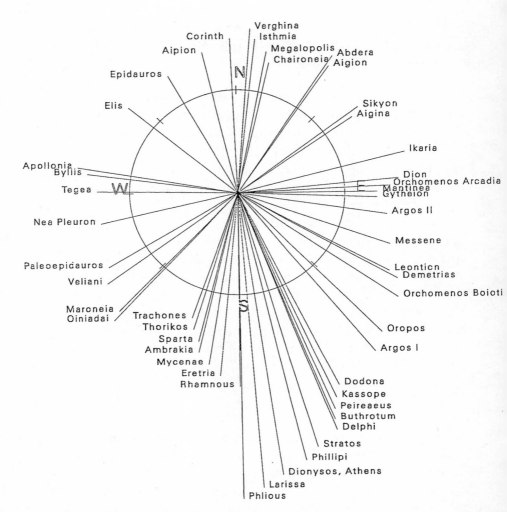

FIGURE 51. *Mainland theatres.*

THE EVIDENCE

The compass roses in figures 51–54 show the 123 theatres and theatre sites from Italy to Asia Minor for which audience orientation can be determined. They are divided into four geographic areas: Mainland Greece, Magna Graecia, the Greek Islands, and Anatolia. Where bearings coincide, lines have been skewed slightly to avoid overprinting. Table 1 gives a tabulation of the four areas.

Place-name spellings are taken from *The Princeton Encyclopedia of Classical Sites*. This may cause some initial confusion (e.g., Katane instead of

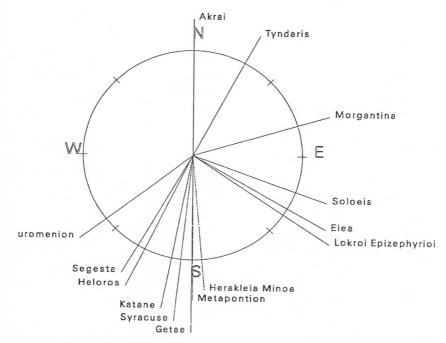

FIGURE 52. *Magna Graecia theatres.*

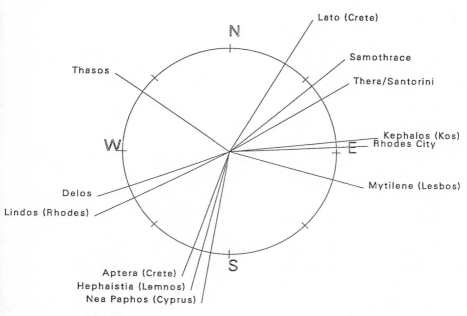

FIGURE 53. *Island theatres.*

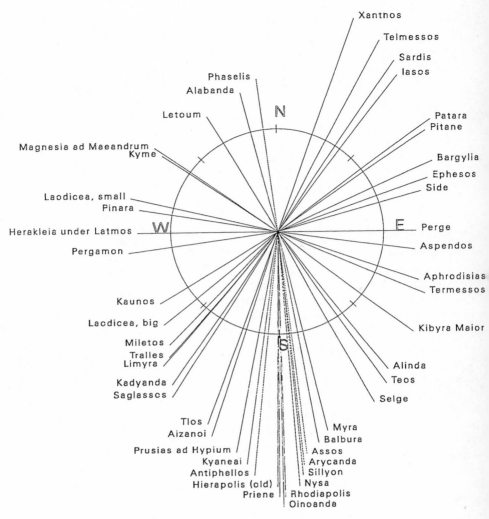

FIGURE 54. *Anatolian theatres.*

TABLE 1. *Audience Orientation by Quadrants*

	North (315–44°)		East (45–134°)		South (135–224°)		West (225–314°)		Total
Mainland Greece	18%	(9)	24%	(12)	43%	(21)	14%	(7)	49
Anatolia	15%	(7)	21%	(10)	48%	(23)	17%	(8)	48
Greek Islands	8%	(1)	42%	(5)	25%	(3)	25%	(3)	12
Magna Graecia	14%	(2)	29%	(4)	50%	(7)	7%	(1)	14
Total	15%	(19)	25%	(31)	44%	(54)	15%	(19)	123

Catania), but it will allow easy reference for those wishing to enquire further about particular locations.

Explanations and Qualifications

Bearings are taken from either Greek sites or Roman theatres built upon earlier Greek foundations. Most were initially constructed in the fourth and third century, although a few are from the fifth; frequent remodeling complicates the problems of dating. Excluded from consideration are theatres totally Roman in origin; four cult theatres (the Kabirion near Thebes, the theatre of Apollo Erethemia on Rhodes, and the small theatres of Messene and Delos);[10] and pre-Greek sites on Crete and Lemnos.

Bearings are not of equal reliability; many are taken from such undoubtedly correct sources as excavation ground plans, but a few are from dubious freehand sketches found in various guidebooks. A large number come from personal observations made at the sites — with declination disregarded, since in this part of the world magnetic north varies no more than two degrees on either side of true north.

Guesswork and approximation are necessarily involved. Theatres at Sardis and Aigina were long ago pillaged, leaving only shaped hillsides to indicate orientation; Aptera and Stratos lie unexcavated, providing only hints of direction. At the isolated mountaintop occupied by ancient Veliani no trace of a theatre is visible, but a modern site plan indicates one in dotted lines. Comprehensiveness, I hope, will compensate for a degree of inexactitude.[11]

The Mainland

Because of their proximity, the islands of Aigina and Euboea are considered with the Mainland (see fig. 51). Three Albanian theatres, Apollonia, Buthrotum, and Byllis, are also included here.

Nea Pleuron is unusual in two features; it is one of the few definitely west-facing theatres in this group; it lies within the walls of the akropolis rather than on an outer slope. The fortification wall served as a backdrop for this small theatre,[12] and it also kept the late afternoon sun out of the audience's eyes.

Four theatres are constructed on level sites using excavation and/or earth-fill to create an artificial slope; the choice of siting here does not depend upon topographic features. These four have their audiences facing around the compass: Mantinea could not have early-morning performances because their audiences would face the rising sun; nearby Tegea would avoid performances in late afternoon because of a westward orientation; Eretria points to the south; and the huge Makedonian theatre at Dion faces northeast. One other theatre constructed on level ground, Metapontum, in southern Italy, faces south.

Magna Graecia

Most of these theatres are Romanized but have Greek antecedents (see fig. 52). In the case of Katane, the bearing comes from the foundation of the original Greek theatre. The large theatre at Locri is totally Roman; the bearing comes from the small, straight-rowed theatre (or possibly a *bouleuterion*) lying adjacent to it.

The Islands

This is the least homogeneous of the four divisions, covering a large area of very separate communities (see fig. 53). Crete is included here since it has only two relevant sites; the bearing for Lato is that of the fourth-century straight-line performance area, not the earlier eighth-century site. Kos, Rhodes, and Lesbos are included here because they seem more political entities, less tied to the Asian subcontinent than the islands of Aigina and Euboea were to Mainland Greece.

Anatolia

Many of these theatres are Roman, but they retain characteristics of their Greek ancestors upon whose sites they were built: all are on hillsides; most have orchestras larger than a semicircle; the *theatron* and *skene* are not connected to form a single architectural unit (see fig. 54). Even such quintessentially Roman structures as the theatres at Side and Aspendos occupy slopes used by earlier Greek theatres. Bearings have been taken from the Roman structures under the assumption that they are similar to those of the Greek originals.

General Observations

The Greek Islands, the smallest of the four groupings, show a preference for east-facing *theatrons* rather than south-facing; Magna Graecia has fewer than average west-facing theatres (see table 1). Aside from these two anomalies, the percentages of theatre headings within each quadrant remain surprisingly constant over this vast range. South is by far the preferred orientation, with west and north both equally undesirable.

In the light of these statistics three questions may be asked: Why is south the preferred direction? What effect, if any, would the position of the sun have on the performances? Can reasons be divined which might underlie the variations in these sitings?

A SOUTHERN EXPOSURE

Vitruvius

Before proceeding with the most answerable of these three questions, Vitruvius' well-known injunction forbidding a southern exposure should be acknowledged:

> We must also beware that it [the theatre] has not a southern exposure. When the sun shines full upon the rounded part of it, the air, being shut up in the curved enclosure and unable to circulate, stays there and becomes heated; and getting glowing hot it burns up, dries out, and impairs the fluids of the human body. For those reasons, sites which are unwholesome in such respects are to be avoided, and healthy sites selected.[13]

Vitruvius' theory and Greek practice diverge sharply here; 54 of 123 theatres (44 percent) lie in the "unwholesome" southern quadrant and almost two-thirds point to the southern hemisphere. Delos, the theatre thought to best fit the Vitruvian model, faces 250° (WSW). Whatever the reasoning behind this Roman architect's advice, it was clearly not rooted in observation.[14]

Warm Bottoms

A statement from the field of modern stadium design offers an obvious explanation for this southern preference: "[American] football is played in cool weather and the sun is welcomed by the spectators."[15] A southern exposure invites the sun to shine upon and warm both spectators and benches in what must have been, in early morning, a stone-cold theatre. Anyone who has sat on a rock for even a quarter-hour on a cloudy day surely remembers the sensation of heat rapidly draining from the body; a stone bench performs the same procedure on the human posterior that a marble slab does for a candy-maker's boiling concoctions.

A cushion would retard this cooling effect by providing insulation, as well as add comfort for the long period of sitting. The wooden benches of almost all theatres during the Classical Age would also have lessened this cooling effect, since wood is a much better insulator than stone.[16] But the southern orientation of most theatres indicates that, even with wooden benches, warmth was a primary concern.

The angle of the sun's rays determines the amount of warmth deposited upon the earth beneath and also determines the quality of light provided for illumination of the performers. Solar heating would have been desirable at Athens' City Dionysia, where plays were presented around the time of the vernal equinox, a period of warmish days and cool nights.[17] On the other hand, the heat of the sun might not be desirable at midsummer.

Compare these sun angles: at the equinox, for all locations in the northern hemisphere, Apollo's chariot first appears due east (90°) and disappears due west (270°). However, between rising and setting, the Sun God follows a curving path (the azimuth) which varies with the latitude. Athens lies at 38° north latitude, sharing the line, incidentally, with Murcia, Spain, and Ouray, Colorado. On 21 March, the greatest height of ascension (GHA) of the sun on this parallel would be 52° above the southern horizon. By comparison, at the summer solstice in Athens, Apollo would begin his drive at 60° (ENE) and disappear at 300° (WNW), achieving a GHA of 75°; on the winter solstice, the ride starts at 120° (ESE) and ends at 240° (WSW), reaching a GHA of only 28° above the southern horizon. Theatres were most likely positioned to provide suitable heat and lighting for the time of year when the most important performances were presented.

Shunning the Sun

American baseball stadia, as constructed before the days of artificial light and extended playing seasons, were intended to house a midsummer sport; consequently, bleachers and their coverings were positioned to provide as much shade as possible for the audience. Similarly, the sun-shunning Greek theatres positioned on north slopes would have been most comfortable in midsummer. (The holes for awning supports drilled into many Greek theatres by the Romans indicate their use at times when the sun was not welcome — but such awnings were not installed until well after the Classic Age. These awnings also indicate a much less democratic environment, since the shade for the rulers necessarily restricted the view for the citizens above.)

THE SUN AND PERFORMANCE

Payers and Players

A maxim of modern stadium design states that any preference in comfort goes to the person in the stands rather than the performer. Most American football stadia of the predome period are laid out on an approximate north–south axis. Given an early afternoon kickoff, the sun's warmth will be equally distributed, and spectators will not be inconvenienced by having the sun in their eyes during a three-hour period. With audience requirements so easily satisfied, some planners, using the sun's azimuth, performed such niceties for the players as canting the stadium slightly from N to S to keep the sun out of the kick receiver's eyes.

However, if a choice needs to be made, it is the player who suffers. The Orange Bowl, a fifty-five-year-old football stadium in Miami, is one of the few built on an east–west axis. Players facing west late in the game, both receivers and defenders, have difficulty seeing the ball when it is in the air. The spectators, however, are not incommoded, since there are no seats in the west-facing end of the stadium.[18]

Similarly, Greek engineers were probably little concerned about an actor's discomfort as he looked into the rising or setting sun; suffering is part of the player's lot. But one cannot imagine a large audience all wearing their traveling hats (*petasoi*), keeping their heads tipped against the sun, and squinting to see what was transpiring in the performing area.

Performance at Dawn

The notion that tragic contests began at dawn's first light has achieved canonical status, although such an arrangement would be next to impossible at the one theatre in four which faces the east. Even at the southward-facing Theatre of Dionysos, spectators seated on the west side of the orchestra would have to contend with the rising sun.[19] The following chapter examines the question of performance time more fully; for the present, suffice it to say that evidence provided by these sitings raises serious questions about the feasibility of a sunrise beginning.

Lighting the Performers

Theatrical lighting by the sun remains an unstudied area, perhaps because it is so rarely used for modern performances. The southward-facing

Theatre of Dionysos seemingly would have serious problems with illumination: at high noon on the equinox, the sun would backlight the actors from a 52° angle rather than the 35–45° front-lit angle that is regarded as standard in the present age. Would there be sufficient bounce light from the *theatron* to keep the actor from being totally rim-lit? [20]

The iris of the human eye adjusts to the brightest object in the field of vision, making objects less brightly lit difficult to perceive. The stark midday contrast between light and shadow might cause problems with visibility.[21] Texas Stadium, situated between Fort Worth and Dallas, illustrates the sun-shadow problem. This semienclosed football stadium (of a design that has not inspired emulation) is oriented NE–SW, a heading originally chosen to allow equal amounts of sunlight to reach all areas of the natural grass playing field. The introduction of artificial turf eliminated any problem of maintaining a suitable playing field, but the unusual siting has left spectators — particularly those watching on television — often partially blinded by the stark contrast between sunlight and shadow. Audience complaints are common at afternoon games.

TOURING CIRCUITS:
A POSSIBLE REASON FOR SITING

While some sites may have been simply ill chosen, the consistent distribution of theatre orientations over the Greek world indicates something other than total randomness. The position and the strength of their only source of illumination and heat were surely studied assiduously — but without slighting such factors as grade, drainage, consistency of soil or rock, traffic patterns, tradition, priestly preferences, proximity to a temple, and perhaps oracular utterances. The ideal sun position might have been compromised to facilitate work on some other aspect of the construction, but it would not have been ignored.

Athens' City Dionysia was an equinoctial festival which included play contests. The usual assumption has been that this Athenian model was followed elsewhere. While it is reasonable to assume that all peoples in temperate zones, Greek and otherwise, celebrated the coming of spring, this celebration did not necessarily involve an Athenian-patterned dramatic event for all Greeks. A spring festival is not necessarily wedded to the equinox; in Eretria and Oreos, the Dionysia was celebrated in February.[22] If the performance of plays was not indissolubly linked to spring revels, possibly the theatres were sited to make best use of the sun at particular times of the year.

In one way, present thinking about the Greeks is not too different from that of London's lord mayor and his alderman, who wrote to the Privy Council in 1597 complaining that play production was "contrary to the rules & art prescribed for the makinge of Comedies eaven amonge the Heathen, who vsed them seldom & at certen sett tymes, and not all the year longe as our manner is."[23] London's city fathers failed to recognize that heathens as well as the citizens of London could not be satisfied with "seldom" entertainments. Athens, in addition to the City Dionysia, presented plays at festivals of the Lenaia, Anthesteria, Rural Dionysia, and possibly the Panathenaia. Apparently noncivic performances were part of the entertainment scene; the Anavysos *chous* fragment, the only picture of a fifth-century play performance, shows an actor in the role of Perseus at a private performance — or possibly a rehearsal for one.

When did acting become a profession? Certainly by the fourth century, as confirmed by references in the orations; but a more likely *post quem* would be the institution of the acting prize at the Dionysia in mid-fifth century. In later ages, one finds amateur performers who make once-a-year appearances; they are generally part of a civic undertaking requiring the efforts of an entire community. The medieval mystery plays, for example, needed a near-total involvement of the town to produce several days of drama. Mardi Gras celebrations held worldwide also require the once-a-year services of countless amateur performers, and the annual dithyrambic contests in Athens involved one thousand amateur chorus members.

But just as dithyrambic *choregoi* were prepared to pay dearly for the finest flutists to accompany their choruses, the three actors entrusted with roles in the tragedies (and a similar number who appeared in the comedies) would have been the best available. Victory in the plays was too important to risk performances by less than the finest, most experienced actors, not amateurs who performed occasionally, nor the fabled "gentlemen actors" who graced the stage only one day a year.

To develop their skills, actors need to perform frequently. Moreover, serious performers would not be content with an annual appearance or two; they would seek to be onstage as often as possible; dedicated actors, heathen or otherwise, never seem to tire of appearing before an audience.

Some Athenian actors of the fifth century may have been able to make a living in Athens, while others might have been either part-time actors with private incomes or perhaps seasonal performers, not unlike the actors in

Britain who subsist most of the year in ordinary jobs in order to appear in the Christmas pantomimes. The numerous waitperson/actors who labor in New York and Hollywood restaurants and bistros are also part-time performers.

Still other actors, adventurous ones seeking fame, money, and audiences, may have gone on the road, and the possibility of touring circuits may provide a logic for the various sitings of the theatres. If professional acting companies visited communities at the same time each year, theatres would have been oriented to best utilize the sun's rays at that time.[24] Festivals might have been positioned to coincide with the arrival of the players.

The earliest information on theatrical travel concerns playwrights, since they were initially of greater importance than actors — although some, like Aeschylus, functioned as both playwright and actor. By the middle of the fifth century, Aeschylus had made two trips to Sicily, writing at least one tragedy while there;[25] at the end of the century Euripides died at the Makedonian court of Archelaus; Agathon, according to the *Symposium*, had been abroad "many years"; in the following century Menander considered making a voyage to Alexandria.

When the first strollers began moving from town to town cannot be determined, but it was probably very early in dramatic history; Csapo and Slater write that "the earliest notices of actors on tour outside of Attica are set at the very end of the 5th c. B.C,"[26] and Taplin finds evidence in the plays of Aristophanes that they were performed outside Athens.[27]

Plato (ca. 360 BCE) has one of his dialogue participants say that first-rate dramatists head straight for the big time in Athens; they "do not go about to other cities at a distance from, and in a circle around, Attica, and make an exhibition there."[28] Aristotle writes disparagingly (ca. 340 BCE) of country players touring from deme to deme,[29] but it is not until the early third century that one finds firm evidence of an organization capable of arranging a complicated touring schedule to the various city-states. Around 277 BCE, a decree by the Council of the Amphiktyonic States, sitting at Delfi, established the "Artists of Dionysos," a guild composed of performers and technicians. The council granted to the *technitai* of Athens "freedom from arrest in war and peace, exemption from military and naval service and, generally, safety of person and property; any offender against them, and even the city in which the offence was committed, being made responsible to the Amphiktyons."[30] In other words, the artists were granted *laissez passer* to tour the territories of the Amphiktyonic states without regard to borders or hostilities.

Actors had traveled freely before this proclamation, much in the manner that athletes routinely crossed battle lines to participate in Panhellenic games. In mid-fourth century, Demosthenes remarked, somewhat jealously, that "Neoptolemus, the actor [serving as an Athenian ambassador to the court of Philip], enjoy[ed] safe conduct under cover of his profession."[31] By the end of the fourth century, such actors as Polus, Theodorus, Thettalus, Athenodorus, and Aristodemus were touring throughout the Greek world. Presumably each festival manager sought the latest plays and the most famous performers for his city; organized touring managed by ancient booking organizations was the obvious way to satisfy the wishes of the many city-states. By the end of the fifth century, "hit" surely became part of the Greek vocabulary, with "star" added shortly thereafter.

The guilds increased; by the third century, major chapters of the Artists of Dionysos were recognized not only in Athens, but in the Peloponnesos, Anatolia, and Egypt, with branches in such places as Euboea and Cyprus. These guilds negotiated with cities to supply personnel for their particular festivals.

Since all of these performances could not have taken place on the equinox, actors might very well have gone on the road with the latest hits (or classic revivals) from Athens or Syracuse or Anatolian Teos, moving from town to town in some scheduled seasonal pattern. If so, theatres were arranged to catch the optimum amount of sun heat and sunlight for the time of year the plays were presented.

CONCLUSION

Of the three questions posed earlier, the one concerning the preference for the south can be most definitely answered: the warmth of the sun was desired in the majority of these theatres. This agrees with the meager information we possess about performance calendars, most of it concerning the City Dionysia at Athens.

The second question concerning the effect of the sun on performance can be partially answered, at least with regard to the audience: spectators will not stare into the rising or setting sun. For many of these theatres, dawn or sunset performances would be impossible.

Regarding the effect of the sun's position on performance, more questions are raised than are answered. The cool, low-angled light of morning produces a different dramatic effect than either the hot down-light of noon or the reddish glow of a hazy sunset. Because front lighting differs from back lighting, the latter can result in serious problems of visibility; bounce light from the *theatron* would improve illumination in both instances. Since the effect of natural lighting on performance has not been studied, research in this area is badly needed.

Considering the reasons advanced for siting, the available-hillside method of choosing does not really square with the seriousness of such an enormous undertaking; it also assumes that the theatre planner lacked an understanding of the sun's seasonal movement, even though this knowledge was the property of every hillside shepherd. The Greeks were familiar with far more complex motions of heavenly bodies than the sun's annual migration; they would not have embarked upon a major civic enterprise involving great expense and years of labor without considering the position of their heat and light source.

The panorama theory is clearly specious, the projection of an indoor people upon the sun-dwelling Greeks. Views are only remarkable if they differ from the everyday; visitors to Wyoming must point out to natives the glories of a routine sunset.

A better approach would be to assume that the ancients knew very well what they were doing when they chose a theatre's orientation. The researcher's task then would be to puzzle out the reasons for their decisions. Further study is needed: computer models showing light and shadow may help to illuminate the problems of illumination.

While an indisputable answer to the "why" of siting cannot be supplied, the evidence presented here leads to some interesting speculations. Were these theatres laid out with different orientations to allow optimum heat and lighting for a major civic event given annually at a certain time of the year? Could this ideal siting have been compromised to accommodate other events happening at different times of the calendar?

Two societies, one British and the other American, have been created to study the ancient trireme, and the Hellenic Navy has commissioned a replica of that vessel. Trials were conducted in 1988; in the summer of 1990, two hundred "short-legged, tough, experienced rowers" from all over the world took the 170 oars of this three-decker, seeking to determine "the most effective style or styles of stroke . . . , the most effective oar design for each tier on the ship," and other questions of propulsion and maneuvering.[32]

This kind of practical, nuts-and-bolts approach to research has never been applied to the study of Greek theatre. Performances staged in the mind's eye have a way of always working to perfection; but real actors and real audiences deal with sun and shadow, heat and cold, rain and wind, dust and mud; these mundane conditions contribute to the shaping of a performance. While the drafting table and the computer may prove helpful, many of the questions encountered here can best be answered by setting up a series of experiments on a literal earthen floor under the light of the actual sun.

NOTES

1. Armin von Gerkan and Wolfgang Müller-Wiener, *Das Theater von Epidauros*, 5.

2. William Bell Dinsmoor, "Archaeology and Astronomy," *Proceedings of the American Philosophical Society* 80 (1939): 95.

3. Scully, *The Earth, the Temple, and the Gods*, 193. All citations are from the second edition (1979).

4. Ibid., ix.

5. Alwyn P. H. Scott, "A Speculative Study," 1–2. Scully also finds analogues between the Greek theatre and Stonehenge (*The Earth*, 22–24).

6. Scully, *The Earth*, 192–194.

7. George E. Bean, *Aegean Turkey: An Archaeological Guide*, 143–144.

8. Scully, *The Earth*, 194.

9. Ibid.

10. The cult theatres at Delos and Messene both have large regular theatres nearby to serve dramatic purposes. The theatre of Apollo Erethemia no longer exists, but it seems to have had a large orchestra and very limited seating. The theatre of the Kabirion has an orchestra almost filled by a large altar, and its seats are scaled to fit juveniles who were participants in this secretive cult, making it unsuitable for drama in the usual sense. Epidauros and Oropos could also be classified as cult theatres since they are attached to healing shrines; they are included here because they are reasonably regular in shape and no other theatres are in the immediate vicinity — although the theatre at Paleoepidauros is not far distant from Epidauros.

11. Errors are always possible. Von Gerkan and Müller-Wiener give bearings down to decimal fractions in their diagram, but a mis-subtraction has transformed the theatre at Eretria from the correct 186° to 174° (see fig. 50). Daria de Bernardi Ferrero's excellent four-volume *Teatri classici in Asia Minore* (Rome: L'erma di Bretschneider, 1966–1974), from which many of these bearings were taken, shows the theatre of Myra to be 168° on one ground plan (plate 40) and 192° on another (plate 41). This discrepancy probably resulted from the reversal of a photographic negative.

12. E. Fiechter, *Das Theater von Oiniadai und Neupleuron*, Antike griechische Theater-bauten, 2 (Stuttgart: W. Kohlhammer, 1931), plate 8.

13. Vitruvius, *De Architectura*, 5.3.

14. Many excavation reports contain such phrases as "the *cavea* opens toward the south in direct violation of Vitruvius' injunction" (Carleton L. Brownson, "The Theatre at Eretria," in *Reprints from The American Journal of Archaeology and The Nineteenth Century* [n.p., 1891], 36).

15. William N. Woodbury, *Grandstand and Stadium Design* (New York: American Institute of Steel Construction, 1947), 7.

16. A 1 inch thickness of limestone has a conductivity of 12.50, while soft wood (fir, yellow pine, etc.) has a conductivity of 0.80. (For comparison, water has a conductivity of 5.50.) This is measured in Btuh per sq ft per °F temperature difference. See M. David Egan, *Concepts in Thermal Comfort* (Englewood Cliffs, N.J: Prentice-Hall, 1975), 50–53.

17. Susan Guettel Cole offers 10 Elaphebolion as the date of the City Dionysia. See "Procession and Celebration at the Dionysia," in *Theater and Society in the Classical World*, ed. Ruth Scodel (Ann Arbor: University of Michigan Press, 1993), 28. The date would have been left flexible enough to allow for vagaries of spring weather and the possibility of rainouts. With a dirt-floored performance area, inadequate storm drains, and a *theatron* serving as a giant semifunnel, lengthy postponements must have been a possibility.

18. A cursory survey of ancient stadia shows no preferred orientation; with events taking place over many hours in different locations on the playing field, determining an ideal sun siting would be impossible.

19. John R. Porter very kindly sat in the Theatre of Dionysos at dawn on 27 and 29 March 1985. These are some of his unedited remarks from a letter of 29 March 1985:

My own impressions: When the sun was out it did get a bit uncomfortable when seated in the western bank of seats — not terribly so, but enough that one needed to shield one's eyes or look away on occasion (although the ancients may have had tougher eyes than I do). It was not like staring into the hot afternoon sun in the summer, however. I got the impression that the viewing was more difficult higher up, but it was hard to tell (and I can't say what effect the eastern bank of seats would have had when it was built up to its complete height). The sun caused no difficulty at all when I was seated in the eastern bank of seats and very little or no difficulty when I sat near the central axis of the theater.

On a more general note, if this spring in Athens is at all representative of a normal spring in antiquity, the ancients were being rather optimistic in counting on a run of nice days this early in the year. Even when it wasn't raining it was often quite overcast, while this morning [29 March] the sun never shone unimpeded for more than 10 minutes or so at any one time. Morning clouds sprang up and shielded it on and off to varying degrees all the time I was there.

20. The plays of the Lenaia, presented in Athens during late January, offer an interesting dilemma regarding sun position. Was the *theatron* (still undiscovered) turned to the south to catch the faint warmth of the sun — while placing the sun, risen to a maximum height of 32° on 21 January, squarely in the eyes of the spectators?

21. Priene and other southward-facing theatres using the Hellenistic *thyroma* stage pose a further problem; given this back-angled lighting, could anything be seen within these roofed and shaded cubicle settings?

22. A. W. Pickard-Cambridge, *The Dramatic Festivals of Athens*, 289, n. 2.

23. Alois Nagler, *A Source Book in Theatrical History* (New York: Dover Publications, 1959), 115.

24. Healing shrines deluged with a continual stream of cure-seeking pilgrims, places

like the Asklepion at Epidauros and the Amphiarion at Oropos, needed to provide some daytime activities after the drug-induced nighttime stupor of the suppliants had worn off. The *theatra* at these places were probably used for some kind of healing ritual, somewhat like modern revivals and camp meetings. It is possible that a repertory company performed almost daily, but there is no evidence to show that any plays were presented at either of these locations.

25. Oliver Taplin dates the Sicilian performance of *Women of Aetna* at 476/475 BCE, earlier than any of the extant tragedies (*Comic Angels*, 2).

26. Eric Csapo and William J. Slater, *The Context of Ancient Drama*, 16.

27. Ibid., 4–7.

28. Plato, *Laches*, 183a.

29. Aristotle, *Poetics*, 1448a.

30. Pickard-Cambridge, *Dramatic Festivals*, 292.

31. Demosthenes, *On the Peace*, 1.109.

32. Trireme Trust USA, *Newsletter* 3 (October 1989).

8

DAWN PERFORMANCES

Three Days in a Row?

The spectators, thousands and thousands of them, begin arriving in the chill hours before the equinoctial dawn; a few torches cast huge shadows over the cavernous *theatron* as they move to their seats. Clutching woolen himations about them, they arrange the cushions that will soften the long sitting as well as insulate them from the night-chilled benches. The spectators are hushed, almost reverential, speaking to each other in low tones. They are not a people given to breakfasting: a few munch on olives and bread, while others tilt their wineskins for a dilute but still warming jolt of the grape. As the first streaks of light appear in the sky at the eastern side of the theatre (near the Stage Right *parodos*), the Watchman appears on the roof, eerily lit by the flaming brazier he carries onstage. While the audience listens to an already familiar exposition, it looks to the southwest, awaiting the flare of a beacon fire on the nearby Pnyx that will signal the fall of Troy.

This, except for the addition of the brazier as a possible lighting effect, represents the standard version of how a day of tragedy began at Athens' City Dionysia; it was a weighty, solemn, devout occasion. Comparisons are sometimes drawn with the sunrise services of a modern Easter; after all, both are spring ceremonials which celebrate the resurrection of a god.

There is one important difference: if the tragedies were to be integrated into the Christian calendar, they would not be placed at the climax of a forty-day period of fasting and penitence; rather, they would join the events that are part of the joyous revelry preceding Lent. Like Mardi Gras, the Great Dionysia was a time of fun. Pickard-Cambridge observes that, following a night of feasting, the initial day of the City Dionysia began with a formal dress-up parade (*pompi*), which wended its way through Athens, with stops at various shrines and temples. After the dithyrambic contests, the *komos*, a more relaxed, informal, and ribald parade or promenade, took place in the evening. "It may be assumed that the procession was enlivened by satirical songs such as were sung on all such occasions at Athens. . . . Naturally, the procession might also be the occasion of such encounters and love-affairs as Menander often took as the starting-point of his plots." [1] *Laissez les bons temps rouler* could as well apply to the spring celebration at Athens as to the pre-Lenten festivities held each year in New Orleans.

To follow a late night of drinking, singing, revelry, and lovemaking with a before-dawn walk to a chilly theatre is hardly the Greek way; sincere Christians may be able to journey from the feast of Mardi Gras to the famine of Lent, but the citizens of Athens showed little appetite for suffering and abnegation.

A more Greek version of their theatregoing is offered by Philochorus, an Athenian who wrote a history of his city-state some time before 260 BCE. In a preserved fragment of his work, he writes of an earlier time when,

> at the Dionysiac festivals the Athenians, after they had finished their luncheon and their drinking, would go to the spectacle and gaze at it with garlands on their heads, and throughout the entire festival wine was served to them and sweetmeats were passed among them; when the choruses marched in they poured out drinks for them; and when they were marching out after the contest they poured again; this is attested by the comic poet Pherecrates [fl. 440–430 BCE], who says that up to his time the spectators were not left unfed. [2]

"Spectacle," that aspect of theatre so denigrated by Aristotle, surely refers to play performance, although the marching choruses may be those of the dithyrambic contests. Regardless of the event, Philochorus' laid-back atmosphere is meant to be applied to "the entire festival."

This version fits the almost-universal pattern of sleeping-in on holidays. The Greeks, as with all societies before artificial lighting obliterated nighttime, normally rose with the sun; but with the celebrations of the previous evening, a later time for arising on the days of tragic competition is likely. Given the comfort-loving, even hedonistic, traits of the Classical Athenians, Philochorus' account better fits the occasion than does the more rigorous early-rising version. The latter would require a sleep-ridden, slightly hungover citizenry to leave their warm beds in the predawn hours, perform an elaborate toilet, don their holiday finery — and then walk some distance to the theatre, where they would sit shivering in the gray dawn as they waited for the sun's rays to warm a wooden but stone-cold theatre.

My personal doubts about a dawn beginning for the tragic contests emerged in the process of doing research for the preceding chapter on theatre orientation, where a survey of 123 theatres revealed that one-fourth of them would have their audiences looking directly into the rising sun and that most of the others (including Athens) would have spectators in east-facing seats also squinting into the sun. While not conclusive, sun-siting problems were sufficient to prompt further investigation. The following pages examine the evidence upon which the dawn performance is based, before proceeding to a conclusion already made apparent by the question serving as the title for this chapter.

Evidence from the Plays

The idea of a dawn "curtain time" originated from a too-literal reading of the dramatically powerful opening scene of *The Oresteia*. Bieber writes: "The tragic performances began at sunrise. This follows from the fact that several tragedies begin with a scene at dawn, for example the *Agamemnon* and the *Andromeda* of Euripides."[3] The Watchman scene of *Agamemnon* does indeed begin at dawn, but in *Andromeda* the reference is to night. The pertinent fragment of that tragedy reads, in literal translation:

> O, holy night,
> How long a drive you are conducting
> Driving your chariot over the starry surface
> Of sacred upper air
> Through most holy Olympus.[4]

This is not unlike the fourth-century *Rhesus*, which begins in the hours of darkness. In the opening lines of that play, Hector exclaims "By what right / do men come prowling *in the night* / across my quarters?" (emphasis added here and in subsequent quotations).[5] This scene was necessarily lit by the sun, but actors and extras probably carried lamps and torches onstage to reinforce the night-time illusion, not unlike Capulet's call for "more torches" to illuminate a night scene in the middle of an Elizabethan afternoon.

Other plays also mention the time of day; Sophocles' *Elektra* and *Antigone* clearly begin at dawn, and Hermes observes the sunrise in the course of his prologue in *Ion*. On the other hand, Euripides' *Elektra* definitely begins at night. Unfortunately, these four plays provide no information about performance times since we do not know whether they were first, middle, or last in order of presentation. However, both *The Eumenides* with its slumbering Furies and *The Trojan Women* with its chorus of sleeping women begin at or near dawn — and both were definitely the last tragedy of the day! *The Suppliants* and *Prometheus Bound* were definitely the first plays performed, yet neither makes reference to time of day. Aristophanes has three of his plays, *Wasps*, *Lysistrata*, and *Clouds*, begin at dawn.

Indeed, a reference to the heavens was such a conventional opening for tragedies that Aristophanes and Menander caricatured these practices in their comedies. Plautus' version of Philemon's *The Merchant* illustrates in the opening speech just how overused this device became: "I'm not going to do what I've seen love-stricken characters in comedy do, when they tell their troubles to Night or Day, to Sun or Moon."[6] Clearly, the Greek playwrights, like Petruchio, could command the heavens, ordering whatever time they chose.

At the Great Dionysia for well over a century, three playwrights each year wrote opening lines for their tragic tetralogies: did more than three hundred plays begin with a reference to an all-too-apparent rising of the sun? As a playwriting technique, it makes better sense to comment upon stage time only when it is markedly different from actual time; Shakespeare has Romeo say, "Night's candles are burnt out and jocund day / Stands tiptoe on the misty mountaintop" when the actual time is fairly late in the afternoon.

How Long Were the Performances?

One common argument advanced for a dawn beginning is that the events of the Dionysia required utilization of all the hours of daylight. Pickard-Cambridge states categorically that "the day's ceremonies began at daybreak,"[7] and adds later: "With performances going on continuously from dawn to evening."[8] That the days of the festival were crowded is undoubtedly true, but dawn-to-dusk play-watching imparts to the ancient Greeks almost superhuman powers of concentration. This was a holiday crowd numbering in the tens of thousands, not a select gathering of dramatic aficionados. The festive Greeks probably gave more attention to the plays than a modern American audience habituated to changing channels at the first twinge of ennui, but probably not as much as today's smaller French audiences, which sit with rapt stillness listening to lengthy renditions of *Phèdre* and other Neoclassic dramas. The more than one thousand plays written for presentation at Athens' Great Dionysia must have been short enough to avoid restlessness in the multitudes.

There are indications that the Athenians attempted to regulate the length of programs at the Dionysia and that in the early days of competition they imposed a time limit on the plays. Aristotle, in a passage that has caused considerable discussion, writes, "As for the limit of its length so far as that is relative to public performances and spectators, it does not fall within the theory of poetry. If they had to perform a hundred tragedies, they would be timed by water-clocks, *as they are said to have been at one time.*" [9] Aristotle's hesitant "as they are said" is somewhat substantiated by the presence of a water-clock in the theatre at Priene. This second-century *klepsydra* is sometimes assumed to have been used for limiting debate during the legal proceedings presumed to have been held in the theatre. This interpretation ignores the clock's dedication to Dionysos, a god never linked with Themis, the even-handed goddess of justice.

Aeschylus may have learned his craft during a period when play length was restricted and in his old-fashioned manner continued to work with a time limit in mind — even after the restriction was lifted. Using the surviving manuscripts as evidence (a risky procedure since they may have been "enhanced" by later ages), one can see that six of his seven plays are nearly identical in length, varying from 1,047 lines to 1,093; only *Agamemnon*, with 1,673 lines, exceeds this apparent limitation. By contrast, plays of the other surviving dramatists were apparently written in an age with no time limit; Sophocles' tragic scripts range in length from 1,278 to 1,779 lines, those of Euripides from 1,055 to 1,693.

Plays were lengthening during the fifth century; the average number of lines in Sophocles' seven tragedies is 13 percent greater than in the seven of Aeschylus. Euripides' sixteen plays (omitting his brief satyr play and the pro-satyric *Alkestis*) contain an average of 9 percent more lines than those of Sophocles. In the absence of a time limit, Athenians most likely controlled the length of the plays by demonstrations of restlessness and lack of attention — or by fruit throwing and foot stamping, Greek equivalents of boos and hisses.

However, efforts were made to limit attendant parts of the day's performance. In the fourth century, Aeschines mentions "laws governing the proclamations in the theatre" and protests the granting of a crown before a performance, at least partly because it lengthened sitting time. [10] In the same century, a specific law forbade citizens using the announcement period in the theatre to proclaim freedom for favored household slaves. The Greeks were not immune to overlong programs.

How long were the performances? The modern tendency with Greek drama is to take only one tragedy and make an evening of it, but the original performances were undoubtedy shorter, for they needed to fit into the day's schedule. Staged without the modern tendency to add pantomime, pause, elaborate picturization, and choreography, an hour and a half should be more than sufficient for the performance of a single tragedy.

A day of tragedy at the City Dionysia followed this order:

1. On opening day, elaborate sacrifices at the shrine of Dionysos, which adjoined the scene house. After the audience had assembled in the theatre, the sacrifice of a piglet (*katharsia*) in a brief ceremony of purification.
2. Proclamations.
3. Three tragedies.
4. A satyr play.
5. During the Peloponnesian War, a dinner break followed by presentation of a single comedy on each of the three days of tragedy.

How long did an audience spend in the theatre? As an estimate, allow a half-hour for the opening-day sacrifice in the sanctuary of Dionysus and an additional half-hour for *katharsia* and proclamations in the theatre, an hour and a half each for the tragedies, a half-hour for the satyr play, twenty to thirty minutes for each of the three scene shifts and the audience's bathroom functions. This gives a total time of seven to seven and a half hours on the first day, and a half-hour less on days two and three; this is about as much attention as could be expected from a mass audience in a partying mood. If activities began at 9:30 in the morning of the initial day, they would have concluded around 4:30 or 5:00 P.M., with subsequent days being a half-hour shorter.

Other Evidence

Pickard-Cambridge cites two passages from fourth-century orators (sources which he has taken from A. E. Haigh's earlier work) in support of a dawn beginning.[11] One of these is inconclusive, and the other may represent unusual circumstances.

In the first, the ever-litigious Demosthenes is heard complaining about being "assaulted by a personal enemy [Meidias] *early in the day*, when he

[Meidias] was sober, prompted by insolence, not by wine, in the presence of many foreigners as well as citizens, and above all in a temple [i.e., the Theatre of Dionysos] which I was strictly obliged to enter by virtue of my office [as *choregos*]." [12] Demosthenes might well have appeared at an early hour in connection with his duties, but just how early hinges upon the word *eothen*, which can mean "from morn," "at earliest day," or "at break of day." The latest edition of this oration (1990) translates *eothen* as simply "in the morning," and the translator suggests that Demosthenes specified morning because it was a sober time, preventing Meidias from pleading drunkenness, a standard defense against the charge of *hybris*.[13]

In the second passage cited by Pickard-Cambridge, Aeschines is heard speaking scornfully of Demosthenes' toadying to the Makedonian ambassadors of Philip II, saying that "he [Demosthenes] placed cushions and spread rugs; and *at daybreak* he came escorting the ambassadors into the theatre, so that he was actually hissed for his unseemly flattery." [14] In another speech, Aeschines further chastises Demosthenes for persuading the *ekklesia* to assign front-row seats of honor to the Makedonians. He also writes that Demosthenes provided "special arrangements [such as] *the placing of cushions and certain watchings and vigils of the night, caused by men who were jealous of him and wished to bring insult upon his honourable name!*" [15] Apparently, Demosthenes anticipated vandalism and spent the night in the theatre to guard his "arrangements." Then he smuggled the ambassadors into the theatre while only a few early-risers were in their seats. This was clearly not a typical situation. If a dawn beginning for the plays was routine, Aeschines would not have bothered pointing out, scornfully, that Demosthenes appeared with the ambassadors "*at daybreak*."

John Gould and D. M. Lewis, who revised the second edition of Pickard-Cambridge's book, added a speech by Socrates as support for the dawn performance: "At present I observe that when a comedy is to be seen, you get up very early and walk a very long way and press me eagerly to go to the play with you." [16] (The revisers admit that this passage may refer to the Rural rather than the City Dionysia, but with the passage's emphasis upon comedy, the Lenaia would also be a possibility.) To follow the chronology of the passage, before the play is to begin, the person has "walked a very long way" to the house of Socrates and talked with him about going a further distance to the performance. Given travel time and Socrates' tendency to consider carefully all aspects of a situation before making a decision, the passage could well support a midmorning beginning for this comedy.

The three passages by Demosthenes, Aeschines, and Socrates are the only ones that might offer support for a dawn beginning of the plays. As can be seen, all are vague enough to admit differing interpretations.

CONCLUSION

The concept of the tragedies starting at dawn almost certainly sprang from a too-literal reading of the first scene from *Agamemnon*. This was undeniably the first play of the day, and anyone reading it has no difficulty visualizing rosy-fingered dawn creeping across the heavens from behind Mount Hymettos. However, this scene demonstrates mainly the skill of the playwright in setting the scene; it is not a reporting of events of the morning. The most convenient parallel situation comes from *Hamlet*, which also begins in the late hours of the night; no one supposes that Shakespeare's audience arrived before dawn for the performance.

Seen through the eyes of the last century, a dawn performance consorted well with the idea that tragedy was an aspect of "religion"; in the nineteenth-century view, enough discomfort and inconvenience was involved to make play-going more than a little expiatory. Almost unnoticed, a breath of Calvinism had crept into the worship of Dionysos.

Once the orthodoxy of a dawn beginning had been established, evidence was shaped to support this premise. In retrospect, it is astonishing just how thin, inconclusive, and ambiguous is this testimony; nothing firmly points to a dawn "curtain time." Statements from the fourth-century orators might provide some support for an early beginning, but they are too weak to stand alone; they can be given various readings. None of the usual discussions pays attention to the *gemütlich* ambience of the festival, which would have precluded anything as disagreeable as rising and sallying forth in the pre-dawn hours.

This is not to say that the tragedies were not serious or that pity and awe did not attend some if not all of the performances. But these plays were limited excursions into the serious; the overall mood of the Dionysia was one of revelry, not gloom. Each trilogy, after all, was followed by a baggy-pants travesty which featured drunken giants, buggered satyrs, cattle rustling, and dirty dancing, all performed by the surpassingly stupid characters so typical of broad farce. The satyr plays terminated any mood of thoughtfulness.

Based upon the evidence available, Philochorus' version of events at the Dionysia looks far more likely than the currently accepted one; his account would permit a pleasant meal with friends, a garlanded stroll to the theatre, and drinks for everybody! The Athenians, after all, were not Spartan; they would have found little pleasure in listening to windy actors by the half-light of a cold dawn.

NOTES

1. A. W. Pickard-Cambridge, *The Dramatic Festivals of Athens*, 61.

2. Quoted in Athenaeus, *The Deipnosophists*, trans. Charles Burton Gulick, V5. 26–27. Athenaeus of Naucratis in Egypt wrote his thirty-volume *The Learned Banquet* around 200 CE, half of which survives. The passage cited, in keeping with the symposium framework of the writing, is part of a lengthy disquisition on drinking habits through the ages. During the fifth century the word *ariston* was in the process to changing meaning from "breakfast" to "luncheon." Given the leisurely pace with which events are unfolding, "luncheon" or perhaps "brunch" is a more probable translation. Eric Csapo, in comments on an early draft of this chapter, adds the following caveat: "The Greek verb used by Philochorus, *aristao*, is very imprecise. Though in the fifth century it usually refers to a meal eaten at midday, its historical meaning, also present in its compounds, refers to a much earlier meal. In fact, so far as I can see the meal referred to can be any meal taken before the main evening meal, the *deipnon*. On a festive occasion one may well break the usual routine of stale crusts dipped in wine for breakfast, and actually consume a larger meal, which could be called *ariston*, despite the fact that it is taken early."

3. Margarete Bieber, *The History of the Greek and Roman Theatre*, 53.

4. Augustus Nauck, *Euripidis Perditarum Tragoediarum Fragmenta*; translation supplied by Helen Bacon.

5. Euripides, *Rhesus*, trans. Gilbert Murray, in *The Complete Greek Drama*, ed. Whitney J. Oates and Eugene O'Neill, Jr., II:351. Present scholarship questions Euripides' authorship of this play.

6. Plautus, *The Merchant*, in *The Complete Roman Drama*, ed. George E. Duckworth, I:493.

7. Pickard-Cambridge, *The Dramatic Festivals of Athens*, 2nd ed., rev. by John Gould and D. M. Lewis (Oxford: Oxford University Press, 1968), 67.

8. Ibid., 272.

9. Ingram Bywater, *Aristotle on the Art of Poetry*, 1451a and commentary. For the inscription on the water-clock at Priene, see F. Freiherr Hiller von Gaertringen, ed., *Inschriften von Priene*, nr. 177.

10. Aeschines, *Against Ctesiphon*, 41–44.

11. Pickard-Cambridge, *Dramatic Festivals*, 65, n.2.

12. Demosthenes, *Against Meidias*, trans. J. H. Vince, 54–5.

13. Demosthenes, *Against Meidias*, ed. and trans. Douglas M. MacDowell, 133 and n. 291.

14. Aeschines, *Against Ctesiphon*, 76. The phrase *hama te hemerai* translates as "with dawn of day" or "daybreak."

15. Aeschines, *On the Embassy*, 111.

16. Xenophon, *Oeconomicus*, 3.7. The Greek *proi* translates as "early in the day," but it can also mean "before daybreak."

RAMIFICATIONS OF THE THREE-ACTOR RULE

While previous chapters have questioned several of the near-sacred absolutes regarding Greek theatre, this one adheres mainly to the orthodox: the three-actor rule for tragedies and satyr plays is alive, well, and not presently refutable. The following pages apply the rule to the extant scripts in an effort to determine its effect on acting and production practices during the Classic period.

Although questioning of Aristotle's historical accuracy has become fashionable of late, no particular doubt has yet been cast upon this assertion in *The Poetics*: "The number of actors was first increased to two by Aeschylus, who curtailed the business of the Chorus, and made the dialogue, or spoken portion, take the leading part in the play. A third actor and scenery were due to Sophocles" (4.1449a.15–19). Assigning very broad dates to Aristotle's statement, the second actor (the *deuteragonist*) would have been introduced sometime after 500 BCE, and the *tritagonist* around 468.

Why limit the number of actors? The simplest answer is that, in a major contest where the outcome is important, firm rules govern the competition. Although a limit of three actors may have reduced expenses for the sponsoring *choregos*, cost would have been a minor consideration; an additional actor or two would have passed almost unnoticed among the enormous expenses of these festivals; one wealthy Athenian equates his "public burden [of] fitting a warship [with] providing a chorus."[1] Aeschylus added a second actor to the original solo performer, Sophocles added a third, and at that point innovations ceased — at least, that is Aristotle's account of the matter.

The thought of heavy-handed rule-making is still often dismissed by literary scholars, as though such restrictions somehow cheapened the art of the drama. Modern criticism retains some echoes of Julius Richter's 1842 proclamation that the poet/dramatist must have total freedom to create:

> In general the tragedians did not write their plays for the actors or the available number of actors. . . . The question of role distribution never influenced the poet in the composition of his plays; role distribution never became an important factor hindering the poet's work. . . . The poets followed their genius; no external factor could force them to write plays that restricted their genius.[2]

This reasoning confuses the poet's solitary labor with the collaborative endeavors of the playwright, who is necessarily immersed in a producing organization. Allotted only three performers, the playwright structures his plot to fit; much of his labor is concerned with such matters as entrances and exits, suitable roles for particular actors, exposition, picturization, suitability of costumes, and wearability of masks. The practicing playwright is more a creature of the stage than the study.[3]

Regulations for Greek competitions differ little from those of high school Interscholastic League one-act play contests held today in the state of Texas. Both contests limit cast sizes; both award prizes to the best actor as well as the winning play. Aristotle's *klepsydra* may well be an ancestor of the stopwatches used in the Texas contests, where disqualification falls upon any play exceeding the prescribed forty minutes.

Aeschylus (523–456 BCE) became a playwright when only two actors were allowed, but he spans the period when rules were changed to allow a third. The chronology of his plays has been confusing because, as Bernard Knox observes, Aeschylus was an old-fashioned dramatist who wrote essentially two-actor plays long after three were permitted.[4] According to the most recent dating, *The Persians* (472 BCE) falls within the two-actor period; but *Seven against Thebes* (467 BCE) and *The Suppliants* (after 468 BCE) are two-actor plays presented during the three-actor period. *Prometheus Bound* (after 468 BCE) can be performed by two actors if one of them is switched for the mute initially playing Prometheus; using a third actor would eliminate this awkward change.

As Knox points out, when Aeschylus structures scenes for three actors, rarely do more than two of them speak. As examples, Cassandra stands mute during her first appearance in *Agamemnon*, speaking only after the other actors have left the stage; in *Elektra*, Pylades remains mute in his first appearance and then, in a following scene, has only three somewhat awkwardly inserted lines. In the latter instance, either the playwright felt required to make some use of this three-actor option or some Byzantine copyist inserted these lines in an effort to give literary life to the silent Pylades. This scene requires the only fast costume change in all of the surviving tragedies; the actor exits as Attendant and returns on the following line as Pylades. In all other instances — except for one in *Rhesus* to be discussed later — lengthy choruses provide adequate time for even the most over-assigned actor to change both costume and mental focus before reemerging as another character. Many classicists object to the suggestion that Pylades' speech is not an integral part of the play's structure; Pickard-Cambridge speaks of "the three tremendous lines assigned to Pylades."[5]

For the great majority of the thirty-two tragedies and one and a half satyr plays, the three-actor rule works very efficiently — although there are exceptions (discussed later). By separating the major roles requiring the almost-total concentration of a single actor from ones which are the Greek equivalent of "Your carriage awaits, milord," the initial distribution of parts can proceed. That the smaller roles would be played by the least important actor is almost axiomatic; this division is confirmed by the scorn Demosthenes heaps upon Aeschines, a rival politician: "You entered the service of those famous players, Simylus and Socrates, better known as The Growlers. You played small parts to their leads, picking up figs and grapes and chives like an orchard-robbing costermonger, and making a better living out of those missiles than by all the battles that you fought for dear life."[6] An interesting variation on the usual lesser importance of the small-part actor is found in Euripides' *Ion*, where much of the comedy is rooted in the Third Actor's portrayals of six wildly assorted roles. This apparent reversal of the actors' hierarchy is discussed in chapter 12.

Almost nothing is known about the actors who comprised the tragic ensembles beyond the fact that they were male and citizens — at least in Athens. Evidently, age was not a factor: the fourth-century actor contemplating his mask in the often-reproduced Würzburg vase fragment is balding and graying; at the other end of the scale, John Winkler suggests that choruses were composed of *epheboi*, twenty-year-olds who were just completing their required military service.[7]

With almost no evidence to work from, one is left with backward-extrapolation, taking what can be gleaned from casting experience in ages past and present. The following "principles" may offer a basis for understanding how the Greeks might have assigned parts to actors.

1. Audiences want to see the most celebrated actor playing the most important part; therefore, the First Actor should be given the main or title role. This would usually be the part with the greatest number of lines.

2. The First Actor would prefer not to break his concentration by being burdened with small parts — except where necessary and then usually after his demise as the principal figure. Being able to limit his concerns to only a single role per play might also increase his chances of winning the prize for best actor, inaugurated around 449.

3. When roles are doubled, a grouping of parts can be sought through vocal similarities: virgins and old men, for example, would have high-pitched voices, and these roles naturally gravitate to a particular actor. Vocal differences had to be important: three actors with the mellifluous sound-alike qualities of today's network radio announcers would have been of little use. The playwright relied upon a vocal palette of differing pitches and qualities to paint his characters. For this, he needed three distinctive voices.

4. In the case of continuing roles, as in the plays of *The Oresteia*, actors are assigned the same parts. Even with identities hidden by masks, experienced playgoers would be capable of distinguishing one player from another and would expect the consistent characterization a single actor would bring to a role.

Using these criteria, the First Actor often emerges with a single character, the Second Actor has one-to-several major roles, while the Third Actor amasses a long list of minor characters. The following are straight-through solo parts intended for the First (occasionally, the Second) Actor — with no doubling: Orestes (in *Orestes*), Medea, Adrastos, Admetus, Kreon (in *Antigone*), both Oedipus roles, Hippolytus, Ion, Creusa, and the Hekubas of *The Trojan Women* and *Hekuba*) — indeed, in *The Trojan Women* Hekuba could not be doubled, for she never leaves the stage.

Sometimes the death of the major character (or disappearance, as in the case of Andromache) allows the "star" to reappear in other, usually minor roles. Antigone returns as Eurydike and Second Messenger; the actor playing Oedipus in *Oedipus at Colonus* makes another entrance as the Messenger who narrates the details of Oedipus' mystical demise; after his suicide, Ajax comes back as Teucer, his half-brother; Evadne immolates herself and is then resurrected as Athena; Herakles' wife dies and comes back as Herakles.

Did the First Actor play leading roles in all four plays on the same day? The answer is probably "yes" — assuming that audiences want to see the most popular actor in the largest, most demanding parts. Actors One and

Two may have quarreled occasionally over roles, but debates about the better part such as one finds with Othello/Iago, or Charles/Joseph Surface, are not present in Greek plays. The utility Third Actor would not have entered such a discussion; he seldom got beyond playing servant and messenger roles in all four of the day's dramas. For the First Actor, this would have been an unbelievably tiring load to carry, but physical and emotional exhaustion at the end of a performance is not an uncommon condition.[8]

The Oresteia offers an opportunity to visualize what a performance day might have been like for a trio of actors. *Proteus*, the satyr play originally performed with this trilogy, has been lost, making it necessary to substitute *Cyclops*, the only complete satyr play. Most if not all of the other trilogies where plots (if not scripts) have been preserved do not have continuing characters; they lack the three-act structure of *The Oresteia*.

The following schema allows the roles of Clytemnestra, Orestes, and Aegisthus to be played by the same actors throughout: the Ghost of Clytemnestra (in *Eumenides*) is, of necessity, played by a different actor during her brief scene. Perhaps a different ghostly voice and presence would not have offended audience sensibilities.

AGAMEMNON

Actor One	Actor Two	Actor Three
		Watchman
Agamemnon	Clytemnestra	Herald
		Cassandra
		Aegisthus

THE CHOEPHORI

Actor One	Actor Two	Actor Three
Orestes	Clytemnestra	Elektra
		Nurse
		Aegisthus
		Attendant
		Pylades(?)

THE EUMENIDES

Actor One	Actor Two	Actor Three
		Priestess
Orestes	Apollo	Ghost of Clytemnestra
		Athena

THE CYCLOPS

Actor One	Actor Two	Actor Three
	Cyclops	
Odysseus		Silenus

Most commentators apportion roles to any readily available actor, being careful to cover all the speaking parts. Pickard-Cambridge, the only twentieth-century author who attempts a complete tabulation of parts for all the plays, sees no problem in assigning the roles of Clytemnestra and Aegisthus to different actors in succeeding plays of *The Oresteia*; he also places unnecessary demands upon the actor playing Clytemnestra, also assigning him the roles of Elektra and Nurse.[9] A. F. Garvie, in his edition of *The Choephori*, shifts Nurse to the Third Actor, but leaves Elektra with Actor Two.[10] This casting is unnecessary and complicates matters by assigning a young girl's soprano role to the actor likely to have a medium-low vocal range.

In the schedule suggested here, the burden of memorization falls most heavily upon the Third Actor, who must learn a total of 1,144 lines, while Actor One has 756 and Actor Two only 670 lines. Presumably, the prestige of playing major roles was more important than time spent onstage in subsidiary parts.

Like playwrights from other times and places, Greek dramatists probably created roles for specific actors. Even such a minor character as the messenger from Corinth in *Oedipus the King* might have been written with the comic talents of a certain performer in mind.

A Greek actor, required to play an assortment of ages and genders, needed a more extensive vocal range than his modern counterpart, but even allowing for this, a grouping of characters by pitch furnishes a logical alternative to the practice of arbitrary slotting. For *The Oresteia*, Actor One would have the lowest voice, Actor Two the mezzo, and Actor Three the highest range. If parts are divided in this fashion, only Athena seems badly placed; although a technical virgin, she would better fit into the middle voice range rather than the high. However, only Actor Three is available to play the part.

Given the limitation of three, a performer would need at times to reach beyond his normal range; one thinks of Laurence Olivier, who transformed his natural tenor to bass-baritone for the role of Othello. Such a range would be needed in *Andromache*, where the actor playing the feminine title role also plays Orestes; the range is even more extreme in *Hippolytus*, where the lovesick Phaedra and the redoubtable Theseus are the same actor. Grouping mature, presumably contralto female roles with those of mature men would seem sensible (while young high-voiced youths and thin-voiced old men fit well with young women). This leads to some interesting speculation: in *The Women of Trachis*, a baritone actor might play Deianira as a low-voiced Amazon and follow with a thunderous Herakles, or a lighter-voiced actor could play a soprano Deianira and conclude with a Herakles speaking in the thin, quavering voice of a dying man, so weak that he enters on a stretcher.

Sex does not provide a basis for assigning roles. As the roles naturally divide, there is no place for a specialized female impersonator, a Classical equivalent of the Kabuki *onnagata*: an actor could not avoid playing both female and male roles. Height would be an advantage in this necessary gender-bending; an actor could not increase his size with platform shoes (*kothurnoi*) until the third century, but a tall actor could shrink to a woman's or old man's size by rounding his shoulders and hunkering down within the robes or rags of his attire. Polyphemus, in *Cyclops*, is giant-sized. In this slapstick comedy, the role was probably played by a speaking actor whose costume concealed the mute figure on whose shoulders he rode. Stilts are a possibility, as shown on one of the black-figure vases, but are more difficult to maneuver.

Nonspeaking tragic children pose no difficulties since mutes are not counted as actors and may be used freely: examples are the young daughters in *Oedipus the King*, Medea's sons, Astyanax in *The Trojan Women*, Eurysaces in *Ajax*, little Orestes in *Iphigenia at Aulis*, and the children of Herakles in *The Herakleidae*. But Euripides, in his search for the pathetic, introduced speaking children, presenting problems in terms of both the three-actor limitation and relative size; audiences would be unlikely to accept a full-grown actor in a child's role.

Three of Euripides' plays have speaking children: *Alkestis*, *Andromache*, and *The Suppliant Women*. A practical solution to this seeming problem is to allow nearby actors or chorus members to utter the children's lines, while the children pantomime the act of speaking. In *Alkestis*, young Eumelus speaks while standing over the body of his mother; since Alkestis has no further lines and the child is positioned at her bier, the masked "corpse" could deliver Eumelus' lines while the child gestures silently. Andromache's son, described several times as "tiny," has some half-dozen lines which alternate with those of his mother as he clings to her side. The actor playing the child's mother might speak the child's lines, alternating them with those of Andromache. In *The Suppliant Women*, lines of the fatherless boys could be given to chorus members who play their mothers.

The Suppliant Women brings up the problem of assigning lines and determining which characters are onstage at a given moment; the original manuscripts contain little indication of who is speaking and offer no guidance at all regarding entrances and exits. Most translators of this play allow the grieving King Adrastus to remain onstage throughout, even though his silent presence would be distracting in scenes where dramatic focus is elsewhere. At one point (often missed by translators) the actor leaves the stage in order to reappear as Iphis, father of the suicidal Evadne.

Evadne, the distraught daughter, presents still another problem for the three-actor limitation, one shared with the guilt-ridden Ajax of Sophocles: both kill themselves onstage, leaving them unavailable for further roles. However, if Evadne's flaming suttee and Ajax's falling (or running) on his sword were placed at the edge of the orchestra, some *trucs du théâtre* would allow Evadne to reappear as Athena and permit Ajax to be reborn as his stepbrother, Teucer — with a mute replacing the dead Ajax in the hastily organized funeral procession. These solutions are made more likely by the taboo against onstage violence, which seems to have held throughout the Classic period; the death agonies of Clytemnestra and Aegisthus, for example, are heard but not seen.

Rhesus presents a particular problem; one scene needs either a fourth actor or a fast costume change. Unlike the usual arrangement, where intervening choruses grant more than adequate time for an actor to switch characters, this play allows only eighteen lines (623–641) for the actor playing Odysseus to transform himself into Paris; then, in Pickard-Cambridge's words, the actor performs "a lightning change back to the costume of Odysseus between 668 and 674."[11] Richmond Lattimore attempts, in his translation, to solve this difficulty by having two characters, Diomedes and Odysseus, "vanish" as Paris enters (642), then proceeding at line 667 to let Athena converse with Diomedes and Odysseus while they are still offstage.[12] While these solutions are possible, use of a fourth actor would supply the simplest solution.

The consensus of present-day scholarly opinion holds that *Rhesus* is the work of an unknown playwright written during the fourth century; Lattimore does not agree: "I now believe that *Rhesus* is the work of Euripides and probably done before 440 B.C."[13] The script's questionable position in the historical canon further complicates efforts to explain the unusual logistics of this scene.

Oedipus at Colonus offers a slight challenge to the three-actor limitation; this play requires the unusual shifting of a role among the three actors, something not encountered elsewhere in the scheduling of parts. This play proceeds in normal doubling fashion until the blind hero goes to his offstage apotheosis: then use of a fourth actor can only be avoided if the role of Theseus is shifted among all the actors — who would need somehow to fuse their individual vocal and physical characterizations.

Actor One	Actor Two	Actor Three
Oedipus	Antigone	A Stranger
		Ismene
		Theseus
	Theseus	Kreon
Messenger		Polynikes
Theseus	(Ismene appears in the final scene as a mute.)	

One piece of archaeological evidence remains to be discussed: a scene by the Capodarso painter apparently pictures a tragic performance on a wooden stage — with *four* actors (*Comic Angels*, 6:11)! Taplin speculates that, in spite of the theatrical setting, this painting might be an example of painterly storytelling rather than a scene from a play.[14] This might picture four speaking actors, or three actors and a mute. Since neither the play nor the subject matter of the scene has been identified, the import of this quartet remains undecided.

CONCLUSION

Conjectures about three-actor exceptions are surrounded by *ifs*. If Pylades' three lines in *Choephori* are the work of Aeschylus, special quick-change costume arrangements must have been made — or a fourth actor was used. If *Rhesus* is a late fourth-century play, possibly the rules had been relaxed sufficiently by that time to allow occasional use of a fourth actor; or if Pickard-Cambridge's "lightning change" is adopted, the scene may represent a poor piece of play construction by an unknown playwright. On the other hand, *if*, as Lattimore maintains, the play is the earliest preserved work of Euripides, either the young playwright had not mastered the technique of actor-switching or he made use of a fourth actor. However, *if* either script was "improved" by later copyists, all bets are off. In *Oedipus at Colonus*, Sophocles may have been experimenting, trying to expand the rules; he was, after all, the innovator who introduced the Third Actor. But a sharing of roles between actors could have been standard practice; one needs to keep in mind that, with only thirty-two scripts remaining from the thousands that were performed, any judgment can have only a limited validity.

Working from a very nonrepresentative selection of scripts, application of the three-actor rule to the tragedies and satyr plays suggests the following probabilities:

1. The almost-total adherence to this rule over a long period indicates a contest with rigid guidelines and procedures.

2. Because the actors were competing for an acting prize, protagonists were provided with long, uninterrupted roles and spared minor-character distractions.

3. Choral passages usually provided actors with adequate time to change from one character to another.

4. Doubled roles may usually be grouped by pitch; in all likelihood, the three actors were selected for differing vocal ranges, from basso to high tenor or countertenor.

Finally, there is every reason to assume that the Greek playwright had the talents of his three actors in mind *before* beginning work on a script and that, like Shakespeare, he wrote parts to utilize the various talents of this company. Most working playwrights are intimately involved in the processes of production, attuned to the needs of flesh-and-blood actors with varying pitch ranges, vocal qualities, personalities, talents — and idiosyncrasies. The Greek playwright was not, as one Ancient wrote of Euripides, a shy recluse who did his creative work in a cave on the island of Salamis.

NOTES

1. Xenophon, *Oeconomicus*, 7.3.

2. Julius Richter, *Die Vertheilung der Rollen unter die Schauspieler der Griechischen Tragödie*, 3–4.

3. Part of the problem here is the homonymic confusion of "write" and "wright." The current *American Heritage Dictionary* (3rd ed.) calls a playwright "one who writes plays," but defines a wright as "one that constructs or repairs something." Perhaps a new word, "playwrighting," would better express the function of the dramatist.

4. Bernard Knox, "Aeschylus and the Third Actor," in *Words and Action: Essays on the Ancient Theatre*.

5. A. W. Pickard-Cambridge, *The Dramatic Festivals of Athens*, 141.

6. Demosthenes, *De Corona*, 262. With a rhetorician's disregard of consistency, Demosthenes also assigns Aeschines the major role of Kreon in Sophocles' *Antigone*, giving the orator an opportunity to recite some words which "Aeschines omitted to quote, though he has often spoken the lines, and knows them by heart; for of course you are aware that, in all tragic dramas, it is the enviable privilege of third-rate actors to come on as tyrants, carrying their royal sceptres" (*De Falsa Legatione*, 247). Perhaps Aeschines was at this time with another troupe and had graduated from Third Actor to leading roles.

7. See John J. Winkler, "The Ephebes' Song," in *Nothing to Do with Dionysos?* ed. John J. Winkler and Froma I. Zeitlin, 20–62.

8. By 341 BCE, according to Margarete Bieber, the assigning of actors was changed so that the three protagonists performed on all three days, each appearing in one tragedy by the playwright of the day. This would have had the effect of leveling the competitive playing field for both playwright and actor in prize competition. (Bieber does not mention appearances in the satyr plays.) See *The History of the Greek and Roman Theater*, 81–82.

9. See Pickard-Cambridge, *Dramatic Festivals*, 137–143.

10. Aeschylus, *Choephori* (Oxford: Clarendon Press, 1986), liii–liv.

11. Pickard-Cambridge, *Dramatic Festivals*, 147.

12. Richmond Lattimore, ed., *The Complete Greek Tragedies: Euripides IV*.

13. Richmond Lattimore, introduction to *Rhesus*, 5.

14. Oliver Taplin, *Comic Angels*, 27–28.

VALIDATION BY AUTHORITY

Margarete Bieber's Comparisons of Hellenistic

and Roman Theatres

Of the many archaeologists who have written about the ancient theatre, Margarete Bieber speaks most directly to the interests of the theatre historian. Almost alone among the diggers-up of ancient civilizations, she shows an obvious concern for the requirements of performance and performer. Chapters in *The History of the Greek and Roman Theater* titled "The Evolution of the Art of Acting," "Scenery and Mechanical Devices," "The Art of Acting at Rome," and "The Influence of the Ancient Theater on the Modern Theater" show clearly her interest in the crafts of play production.[1] She was a theatre aficionado and did not hesitate to make comparisons between ancient satyr dramas and the "interplay of jest and earnest in religious festivals found in the plays performed by the inhabitants of the island of Bali" (17). Bieber was concerned with the practical aspects of staging; she took the time to diagram actor entrances for Sophocles' *Oedipus the King* (59) and to compare staging arrangements for "Asiatic" and "Athenian" productions of Menander's *The Arbitrants* (123). While many researchers rely upon an incomplete knowledge of production mechanics, often seeming uninterested in backstage operations, Bieber exhibits a lively curiosity about both modern and ancient worlds of theatre. More than fifty years after the original publication, her *History* remains a basic text for anyone interested in exploring the Classical theatre.

It is ironically unfortunate that Bieber's writings are so well regarded that they have achieved almost scriptural authority; nowhere is this more evident than in the catechizing of her one-page list of "differences between the Greek-Hellenistic and the Roman theater" (189). These fourteen points have been memorized as articles of faith by generations of doctoral students facing the rigors of comprehensive examinations, and neophyte professors of theatre history (myself included) have unhesitatingly passed along these comparisons to students searching for solid ground from which to view a six-century continuum of gradually evolving theatre structures. In an area where so much of the evidence is either incomplete or contradictory, Bieber's clarity and assertiveness provide a small but firm island in a sea of quicksand.

A recent article on a Roman theatre in Spain shows just how scriptural her opinions have become. Apparently proceeding from Bieber's pronouncement that Roman theatres were built mainly on level ground, the author states that "unlike most Roman theatres, it [Sagunto] is not entirely free-standing: The seating section, the *cavea*, is carved into the rock of the hillside. The theatre was built in the hillside in part because there was not a large area of level land on which to construct a free-standing theatre within the city."[2] This tortuous reasoning brings the Sagunto site into conformity with Bieber's dictum that Roman theatres are "mostly built on high substructures from level ground" (189), but it ignores archaeological evidence showing that, of fifteen Roman theatres on the Iberian peninsula, only the ruins at Zaragoza (Caesaraugusta) reveal the series of radiating risers necessary to support a *cavea* raised above level ground.[3] Apparently, the pronouncements of such an authority as Bieber are to be honored unquestioningly — in spite of evidence to the contrary.

The purpose of this chapter is not to carp at minor errors in Bieber's scholarship, but to provide an example of just how readily the pronouncements of recognized authorities are accepted as truth. The following pages examine the evidence supporting three of Bieber's fourteen points of Hellenistic-Roman comparison (189) and suggest possible revisions: of the remaining eleven points, several are in need of qualification, but the arguments for restudy cannot be made as clearly.

HELLENISTIC	ROMAN
[1A.] Entrance for all spectators is through the *parodoi* and the orchestra leading to the radiating staircases.	[1B.] Entrance for the public from level ground is through outer vaulted entrances, staircases, vaulted and open passageways.

[2A.] The auditorium is built against a hillside and therefore has no outside facade.

[2B.] The auditorium occasionally is also laid on a hillside (Vitruvius, 5.3.3), but mostly built on high substructures from level ground with a rich facade, a colonnaded gallery, and sometimes shrines on top.

[3A.] The orchestra is a full circle.

[3B.] The orchestra is a half circle.

1A. Entrance for all [Hellenistic] spectators is through the parodoi *and the orchestra leading to the radiating staircases.* Surely, no manager of a well-run festival would allow a holiday horde of many thousands to tramp through backstage areas and across the orchestra during those final, harried moments before showtime. Visualize, if you will, a wine-filled spectator wobbling across the orchestra during the archon's dedicatory address or a late-arriving Greek dodging around Agamemnon's chariot on the way to a seat!

Bieber's statement is contradicted by the remains of Hellenistic theatres, all of which had entrances on the sides; many also had them at the rear. In Athens, a literal road ran through the middle of the *theatron* at the cross aisle (*diazoma*), a major thoroughfare connecting the Agora on one side with the Street of the Tripods on the other. These wide passageways were surely used for audience traffic.

Only one scrap of evidence can be found that points to an audience entrance through the *parodoi*: this is testimony given in relation to the desecration of the herms during the Peloponnesian War. A witness speaks of overhearing a conversation as he lurked in the sanctuary of Dionysos, near "the gateway of the theatre of Dionysos."[4] The sanctuary lay just downslope from the theatre, and there would be, in all likelihood, a passageway between the two; it would have been small, permitting priests and city fathers to make a ceremonial entrance after sacrificing in the sanctuary. Tens of thousands of spectators could not have squeezed through two *parodoi* measuring a little over eight feet in width.

1B. Entrance for the [Roman] public from level ground is through outer vaulted entrances, staircases, vaulted and open passageways. Staircases are standard features of Roman theatres, whether they were constructed on a hillside or on level ground, but many Hellenistic theatres also had staircase entrances: Epidauros and Delos are examples. The "vaulted entrances" (*vomitoria*) are typically Roman, but they are also used in the Hellenistic theatres at Sikyon and Alinda.[5]

2A. *The [Hellenistic] auditorium is built against a hillside and therefore has no outside facade.* Except for the theatre at Eretria, where the builders ignored a nearby hillside and built their *theatron* on dirt excavated from the orchestra, Greeks used natural slopes where available. Note should be taken, however, of four other Hellenistic theatres that were constructed on artificial mounds of earth piled on flat plains: Mantinea, Tegea, Eretria, Dion, and Metapontum. Builders at Chaironeia, fourth-century Argos, and many other locations found it necessary to mound up seating embankments at the sides of the orchestras if nature had not provided a natural bowl. The Greeks created their own hillside if one was not available.

2B. *The [Roman] auditorium occasionally is also laid on a hillside (Vitruvius, 5.3.3) but mostly built on high substructures from level ground with a rich facade, a colonnaded gallery, and sometimes shrines on top.* The "occasionally" and "mostly" are not found in the cited passage of Vitruvius; in fact, the Roman architect seems to be saying the opposite: "The foundation walls will be an easier matter if they are on a hillside; but if they have to be laid on a plain or in a marshy place, solidity must be assured and substructures built in accordance with what has been written in the third book, on the foundations of temples."[6] Because first and favorable consideration is given to hillsides, with level-land locations relegated to sites of last resort, a better reading would be that Vitruvius regarded a hillside as the preferred location for a Roman theatre, with level ground used only when a hillside was not available.

Bieber apparently based her "level ground" statement on three freestanding theatres built on Rome's Campus Martius, the "marshy plain" that led Vitruvius to advise care in providing solid foundations. Placed on the floodplain of the Tiber *only* because there were no other sites available, these theatres represent exceptions, not the norm. According to John Arthur Hanson, "The theatres of [the Emperors] Pompey and Marcellus and Balbus (especially that of Pompey) could not have been built on these hillsides because they included as parts of their plans 'public amusement parks' of such an extent that the level and little-inhabited Campus Martius was the only practical ground on which to build them."[7]

Some support for Bieber's level-ground contention may be found in two other level-land theatres not far distant from Rome. Ostia, the ancient seaport of the capital, sat on the extensive flat land of the Tiber's delta. There is also the still-buried (by Vesuvius) theatre at Herculaneum, some one hundred kilometers from Rome, which has been tunneled into sufficiently to determine that it sat mainly upon level ground; however, the enfolding layers of pyroclastic mud from Vesuvius make it difficult to determine topography and its effect on siting.

Although the Romans loved engineering challenges, they preferred a relatively easy hillside foundation over the building requirements of a flat plain. However, when expansion of an existing *cavea* became necessary, the Romans added an above-ground, free-standing extension at the rear of the existing hillside seating: Kaunos, Myra, Aizanoi, Perge, and Side utilized a natural slope only as high as the *diazoma*. This preference for hillsides was based partially on the fact that most Roman theatres were built upon reused Greek sites; but when the city of Hierapolis moved its hillside theatre to a new location during Roman times, the builders rejected readily available flat land in favor of yet another hillside. In all of Anatolia there is only one theatre, Tlos, that appears to have been built on level ground.

In Mainland Greece there are no free-standing Roman theatres; the purely Roman theatre at Nikopolis occupies a hillside, as does the *odeion* of Herodes Atticus, in Athens. In Britain, the Roman theatre at Verulamium, looking suspiciously like an adaptation of a Cornish round, sits on a plain — but is built primarily on a piled-up earthen doughnut.[8] Of the European theatres examined, only the previously mentioned theatre at Zaragoza may have been free-standing. At Timgad, in North Africa, recent excavation has revealed that the north section of the *cavea* rests upon risers, rather than being entirely hill-supported as previously believed. Contrary to Bieber's statement, free-standing theatres were built only when a suitable hillside was not available.

Bieber was correct when she specified a "rich facade" for these theatres. The Romans, with their horror of the artistic void, sought to fill every space with ornamentation: scene houses were elaborately adorned with columns, arches, niches, statues, and elaborate moldings; the side walls of the *cavea* received similar treatment, as did the rear walls where they rose above ground. No evidence, however, indicates that level-land theatres were constructed to provide greater opportunities for the display of Classical gingerbread.

3A. The [Hellenistic] orchestra is a full circle. At this juncture, perhaps more than any other, one wishes that, like Darius in *The Persians*, Professor Bieber could be summoned from the shades and asked, "Whatever did you mean by 'full circle'?" In her time, only the remains of the theatre of Epidauros possessed a full circle delineated by a stone boundary. Since her death, only the Hellenistic theatre at Argos has disclosed another similarly marked circle, one previously hidden beneath a later Roman scene house.

Although the theatres at Eretria, Assos, Oeniadae,[9] Piraeus, and Athens possess sufficient room to inscribe a complete circle, the configuration of the remains emphasizes a U-shaped rather than a circular orchestra. (Bieber calls this shape "horseshoe.") Moreover, Vitruvius, the ultimate source of the concept, does *not* specify a complete circle for his Greek theatre; he shows the front of the "proscaenium" laid along the side of a square inscribed *within* a complete circle.[10] The increasing number of rectangular and trapezoidal orchestras that have come to light further obscure the meaning of "full circle."

3B. The [Roman] orchestra is a half circle. It would be more accurate to say that the Roman orchestra *tends* toward a half circle. Although Bieber is supported by strict semicircles with a diameter drawn at the edge of the *pulpitum* in the theatres of Pompey, Fiesole, Alinda, Ostia, Pergamum, and Minturnae, even more theatres have orchestras which are built U-shaped in order to include side entrances into the orchestra: Taormina, Orange, Aspendos, Patara, Assos, Aphrodisias, and Magnesia are examples of these. Still others have the orchestra extending beyond a semicircle: Miletus, Sagalassos, Myra, Laodicea, Side, Selge, Lymira, Efesos, Iasos, Kibyra, Oenanda, Stratonikea, Termessos, Telmessos, Alabanda, Priene, Heraclea al Latmos, Kyanae, Balbura, Antiphellos, Pinara, Arykanda, Kadyanda, Letoon, and the anomalous British theatre at Verulamium. Further variation is provided by Roman theatres of Patara, Hierapolis, Prusias ad Hypium, Nysa, Kaunos, Perge, and Rhodiapolis, all possessing orchestras large enough to encompass a full circle though not defined by curbing. As if that were not enough variety, Spain has two theatres, Segobriga and Sagunto, whose orchestras are *distinctly less* than a semicircle. To add further confusion to this picture, Richard Green writes the following by e-mail (6 June 1998) about his excavations on the island of Cyprus: "The [Greek] cavea at Paphos is a semicircle (in fact 181 degrees) and seems on present evidence to be one of the earliest if not the earliest known (there are reasonable grounds for believing that it was constructed ca. 300 BC)."

With so many varieties of shapes at hand, Bieber's generalization clearly stands in need of refinement and qualification.

Other Comparisons

Of the remaining eleven comparisons, several others merit a second look. The statement that Hellenistic theatres are "built in sanctuaries" (189) would be true of Oropos, Delfi, and Epidauros, where the theatres were part of religious complexes. Athens, Thorikos, and Gytheion might also fit into this category, since they had temples adjacent to their theatres. However, further study would likely show that most theatres, while involving some religious ceremony, cannot be called full-blown "sanctuaries" in the same sense as the healing and oracular complexes named above.

In another comparison, Bieber states that "Greek performances are literary events" and that the Romans preferred "shows catering to the taste of the public" (189). This assumes that Athenian holiday throngs numbering in the tens of thousands came to the Great Dionysia wearing the mantle of Aristotle, concerned not so much with having a good time as with winnowing philosophic wheat from the chaff of theatrical spectacle. One wonders whether such a judicious mass audience was ever assembled.

CONCLUSION

In the examples considered here, Professor Bieber's generalizations are hasty, based upon misreadings of the limited information available. In these instances, her writings are in need of modification or revision. This is not to tarnish the respect that her scholarship has earned: many publications stand as enduring monuments to her industry, perception, curiosity, and powers of analysis.

The point of this discussion is to show how easily the ruminations of recognized authorities can be transformed into canonical utterances. Bieber, Pickard-Cambridge, Dörpfeld, Pollux, Vitruvius, Aristotle — indeed, all the esteemed figures of past and present scholarship — should be honored for their accomplishments, but their views must be subject to periodic re-examination. Reverence needs to be tempered with skepticism: in the words of G. J. Renier, "Clearly, in using accepted history we must make sure that it still deserves to be accepted. It is a gift-horse that cannot be looked too often in the mouth." [11]

NOTES

1. Subsequent references are given interlinearly.

2. Yvonne Shafer, "A Roman Theatre in Restoration," *Theatre Design and Technology* 28 (Winter 1992): 12.

3. Simposio El Teatro en la Hispania Romana, Institución Cultural Pedro de Valencia, *El teatro en la Hispania Romana* (Badajoz: 1982).

4. Andocides, *On the Mysteries*, in *Minor Attic Orators*, 1:371.

5. See Thomas D. Boyd, "The Arch and the Vault in Greek Architecture," *American Journal of Archaeology* 82 (1978): 83–100.

6. Vitruvius, *De Architectura*, 5.3.3.

7. John Arthur Hanson, *Roman Theater-Temples* (Princeton: Princeton University Press, 1959), 48. Of these three theatres, Balbus is undiscovered, scant remains of Pompey's theatre can be seen in various Italian basements, and the facade of Marcellus has been incorporated into an apartment house near Capitoline Hill. Hanson mentions (48) that there was also a hillside theatre on the Capitoline slopes.

8. Kathleen K. Kenyon and Sheppard S. Frere, *The Roman Theatre of Verulamium, Official Guide* (n.p.: n.d.), not paginated.

9. Heinrich Wirsing, the artist who sketched many of Bulle's reconstructions, has shown the Oeniadae theatre with a complete stone circle; Bulle's ground plan shows a circle mainly in dotted lines: Heinrich Bulle, *Untersuchungen an Griechischen Theatern* (Munich: Verlag der Bayerischen Akademie der Wissenschaften, 1928), plates 14 and 16.

10. Vitruvius, *De Architectura*, 5.7.1. Bieber was very much aware of what Vitruvius had to say about orchestra shape, writing that "the *proskenion*, therefore, intrudes upon the basic orchestra circle by the full amount of its projection before the main scene-building" (127).

11. G. J. Renier, *History: Its Purpose and Method*, 92.

11

VALIDATION BY REPETITION

The Menander Reliefs

While some assumptions regarding Greek theatre are rooted in the pronouncements of authority figures, others have grown from tentative speculations elevated to the status of "fact" by nothing more substantial in the way of evidence than being frequently cited. This brief chapter examines the process by which the small, unlabeled high reliefs at the Vatican (fig. 55) and Princeton Museums (fig. 56) have become firmly established as portraits of the New Comedy playwright Menander.

Earlier in the century, scholars were not so certain about this identification. As late as 1935, Lucien Dubech placed a dubious "Ménandre(?)"[1] beneath a picture of the Vatican relief, and the majority of his contemporaries expressed similar reservations. This seemingly justified question mark gradually disappeared during the following years — not, however, as the result of newly discovered confirming evidence. On the contrary, any lingering doubt was swept away by a deluge of positive but unsubstantiated attributions: if Bieber, Pickard-Cambridge, Webster, Brockett, Margot Berthold, Richard Green, Phyllis Hartnoll, and a host of others confidently asserted that these sculptures were indeed of Menander, how could anyone harbor doubts?

The identification of these figures is based upon the slimmest of evidence. Gisela M. A. Richter, author of a monumental three-volume *The Portraits of the Greeks*, succinctly states the pro-Menander case: "The presence of three comic masks and other attributes show that the seated figure must be a comic poet, and therefore, perhaps, the most celebrated of them, Me-

FIGURE 55. *"Menander" relief: the Vatican version. Courtesy of the Monumenti musei e gallerie Pontificie.*

nander."[2] By extension, the woman in the Vatican version becomes either Glykera, Menander's fictional girlfriend, or perhaps one of the Muses.

Richter's progression from "show" to "must" and a concluding "therefore," followed by a muted "perhaps," leaves room for more than a little doubt about who — or even what — is pictured in these reliefs. The following pages reassess this presently well-established identification, hoping to learn whether the question mark should be returned to citations of these works — or even if an "unknown" label would be more appropriate.

THE RELIEFS AS EVIDENCE

The latest edition of *Monuments Illustrating New Comedy* places the creation of both sculptures between 150 and 50 BCE.[3] The seated figure of the Vatican wears a restored nose, while its Princeton counterpart required a resculpting of the entire head above the mouth; one assumes that the Vatican version was used as a model for this restoration (fig. 57). Because they were unearthed in less than pristine condition, some beginning caution needs to be exercised.

FIGURE 56. *"Menander" relief: the Princeton version. Courtesy of the Art Museum, Princeton University; Museum purchase, Caroline G. Mather Fund.*

Richter states that the Princeton version, originally part of the Stroganoff Collection, is a "replica" of the Vatican relief,[4] but the author and revisers of *Monuments Illustrating New Comedy* are less certain: "It is difficult to know if *b* (Princeton) or *a* (Vatican) . . . more directly reflects the archetype."[5] There is also a partial version of these reliefs showing only the seated figure with generalized features in Berlin's Staatliche Museen; all three of these are believed to be copies of a now-lost original.

Seated Portraits

The posture offers some justification for identifying the seated figure as New Comedy's leading playwright, since this was typical of Menander portraiture. The base for an early third-century BCE statue of the dramatist, proportioned for a seated figure, presently rests under a tin roof near Athens' Theatre of Dionysos, and a similar seated-figure base labeled "Menandros" was found near the theatre at Eretria. In addition, there are seated Menan-

FIGURE 57. *The Princeton relief: a closeup showing the reconstruction.*

ders complete with identifying labels in a mural at Pompeii (fig. 58) and in a much later mosaic from Antioch (fig. 59).[6] The playwright is called "crippled" in several late Classical sources, offering the possibility that the seated pose may have resulted from some physical difficulty. It may be significant that there are no standing representations of the playwright; one is reminded of the seated statuary of polio-ridden Franklin D. Roosevelt.

FIGURE 58. *The Menander mural: Pompeii. Courtesy of Pietro Giovanni Guzzo, Soprintendenza Archeologica Pompei.*

FIGURE 59. *The Antioch mosaic. Courtesy of the Art Museum, Princeton University; gift of the Committee for the Excavation of Antioch.*

The pose, however, does not offer any certainty about the identity of these seated reliefs: although the surviving Menanders are all seated, not all seated figures are necessarily Menanders. A late fourth or early third-century low relief from the west slope of the Athenian akropolis shows a seated playwright or actor wearing a very un-Menandrian beard.[7]

Whether some of these unlabeled theatrical figures represent playwrights or actors is debated. Two Roman murals with seated figures and masks are presumed to be actors: fig. 60 shows a man in half-clad condition similar to the "Menander" reliefs; he is contemplating a tragic mask; fig. 61 pictures an actor still wearing his stage costume; a woman reminiscent of the presumed "Glykera" gazes at a tragic mask, while another actor changes costume in the background. Both of these murals show only one mask, as would be expected when a First Actor performs a tragic role; as seen in chapter 9, the tragic protagonist frequently plays only a single role.

THE MASKS SHOWN IN THE RELIEFS

The two masks lying on the small tables are identified in Webster as (#35) second false maiden, and (#4) long-bearded, wavy-haired old man; the one held by the seated figure is probably (#11) the dark young man. According to Richter, the presence of more than one mask indicates that the seated

FIGURE 60. *A Roman actor and mask: Naples.*

man is a dramatic poet. Her reasoning ignores one of the basic purposes of wearing masks: they enabled the actor to play more than one role. The three characters shown here, falling within a restricted vocal range as suggested in chapter 9, are more likely the different roles that an actor performed in a particular play.

FIGURE 61. *A Roman actor and a woman with a mask: Naples (wall painting). Naples.*

THE SCROLL

The title "dramatic poet" is given to the man in the Princeton and Vatican reliefs mainly because a scroll dangles over the edge of the table. In this interpretation, a dramatist is examining — or communing with — the mask of a character from one of his plays, while other masks lie on the table. Playwrights are usually depicted with scripts alone, not with masks. The Pompeii mural has a labeled Menander holding a script (fig. 58); a standing Sophocles in the Vatican has a *cista* of scripts at his feet (figs. 62 and 63); the playwright pictured in a third-century CE Tunisian mosaic has a similar basket of scripts beside him, while a presumed actor on his left holds a mask (fig. 64).[8]

Since playwrights and actors are usually depicted with the specific tool of their trade, scripts or masks, some confusion is engendered by the Vatican

FIGURE 62. *Sophocles: the Vatican. Courtesy of the Monumenti musei e gallerie Pontificie.*

FIGURE 63. *Sophocles' cista of scripts.*

FIGURE 64. *A playwright and an actor: Hadrumetum. From Mohammed Yacoub*, Chefs-d'oeuvre des musées nationaux de Tunisie. *Tunis: Maison Tunisienne de l'Edition.*

and Princeton reliefs, which contain both script and masks. However, the masks dominate by number and compositional focus.

ACTOR RATHER THAN PLAYWRIGHT? A REINTERPRETATION

It is more likely that the seated person in these two reliefs is not a playwright but an actor studying the mask of the character he is to play next, absorbing its personality just before going onstage. This approach to characterization is still employed by Kabuki and Noh actors, who pause in the

FIGURE 65. *An actor with a comic mask and script. Courtesy of the J. Paul Getty Museum.*

Mirror Room to contemplate their image before making an entrance; I have observed a Noh actor on an American tour who, lacking a backstage mirror, contemplated his mask in the manner of the figure in the reliefs.

The half-dressed condition of the figure, similar to that in fig. 60, can easily be interpreted as showing an actor in the middle of a costume change.

The woman in the Vatican relief and the kneeling woman in fig. 61 are probably dressers, but, considering the well-attired and coiffed appearances of both women, they might also be Graeco-Roman groupies with backstage passes. The scroll hanging over the table edge, to judge by its small size, is an actor's part, one kept at hand for a quick refresher before going on-stage. In similar fashion, the funerary portrait of an actor contemplating an old man's mask shows a writing tablet or scroll lying beside his chair (fig. 65).

BUT WHAT DID MENANDER LOOK LIKE?

Overwhelming all these points regarding identification and interpretation is the fact that the square-faced, rather fleshy individual of the Vatican and Princeton reliefs bears little resemblance to the lean, patrician Menander portrait busts that are found scattered through the world's museums (fig. 66). These unlabeled busts have long been identified as Menander, although for many years a small but vocal group has insisted that they were of Vergil.[9] The Getty's fairly recent acquisition of a tiny Roman bronze (fig. 67) with a faint "Menandros" inscribed on its attached base has, according to Jiri' Frel, "settled some eighty years of discussion about the identity of the man surviving in about fifty copies."[10] Although these heads are not totally uniform,[11] there are sufficient similarities to give a reasonably clear image of the *vrai* Menander. Clearly, the portrait busts and the two reliefs do not picture the same person.

One other point of difference: most of the portrait busts show a head tilt characteristic of a person with vision problems, who must tip his head to bring together the double images associated with a condition known as torsonal diplopia. Menander was thought to be cross-eyed;[12] where pupils are incised or otherwise shown (fig. 68, Lesbos), this condition is present. It is interesting to note that the "unknown" playwright of fig. 64 is cross-eyed and may picture Menander choosing the comic mode over the tragic one. Marion True, the Getty's curator of antiquities, observes that the pupils of the bronze "do indeed show a small misalignment; the proper left pupil is directed slightly more inward than the right."[13] The blank-eyed man pictured in the Vatican relief, on the other hand, has a level gaze, lacking the head tilt characteristic of torsonal diplopia (fig. 69).

FIGURE 66. *Menander. Courtesy of the J. Paul Getty Museum.*

FIGURE 67. *The labeled Menander bronze. Courtesy of the J. Paul Getty Museum.*

FIGURE 68. *Menander: Lesbos.*

CONCLUSION

According to Richter, the many portrait busts scattered around the world show "a sensitive person, . . . with plentiful hair, an oval face, a high forehead that bulges out in its lower part, lean cheeks, finely curving lips, a thin, straight nose slightly curving below the bridge, a small, round, rather prominent chin with a pronounced groove between it and the lower lip, and a slender neck with a prominent Adam's apple."[14] This description does not fit the rather dough-faced individual pictured in the Vatican relief. One must conclude that the "Menander" label applied to this seated figure results from continued but undocumented citings by many writers; what began as a speculation has turned into a "fact" unsupported by evidence.

While the correction of this misidentification may lack the significance of Oliver Taplin's reassessment (in *Comic Angels*) of the historic position of the *phylakes* vases, it may serve as a paradigm illustrating the process by which conjectures become a part of the historical record. In similar fashion, other tentative speculations about the Greek theatre have metamorphosed into historic fact; something need only appear in print a sufficient number of times to become canonical.

FIGURE 69. *"Menander" in full face: the Vatican. Courtesy of the Monumenti musei e gallerie Pontificie.*

NOTES

1. Lucien Dubech, *Histoire générale illustrée du théâtre*, 1:111.

2. Gisela M. A. Richter, *The Portraits of the Greeks*, 2:329.

3. T. B. L. Webster, *Monuments Illustrating New Comedy*, 2:170.

4. Richter, *Portraits*, 2:229.

5. Webster, *Monuments*, 2:170.

6. The other figures in this mosaic are labeled "Comedy" and "Glykera." "The man's face is only a conjectural portrait, but the scene documents the legend of Menander's love for Glykera, which was widespread in antiquity" (Frances F. Jones, "Antioch Mosaics in Princeton," *Record of the Art Museum, Princeton University* 40 [2] [1981]: 4).

7. G. W. Elderkin believes that this figure, in spite of the beard, is Menander. See "Two Mosaics Representing the Seven Wise Men," *American Journal of Archaeology* 29 (1935): 92–111, fig. 22. Margarete Bieber, on the other hand, identifies the man as an actor (*The History of the Greek and Roman Theatre*, 82).

8. Margaret A. Alexander, co-director of the *Corpus of the Mosaics of Thunisia*, which toured American museums a few years ago, has re-examined the mosaic; finding no evidence of reworking, she writes that "the Sousse poet seems to me to be cross-eyed." Personal letter, 2 August 1991.

9. See Rhys Carpenter, "A Contribution to the Vergil-Menander Controversy," *Hesperia* 20 (1951): 30–44 and figs. 19–23.

10. Jiri' Frel, *Greek Portraits in the J. Paul Getty Museum*, 34. Frel dates this bust between the end of the first century BCE and early first century CE.

11. See Richter, *Portraits*, 3: figs. 1514–1643.

12. Suidas, *Suidae Lexicon*, ed. Ada Adler, s.v. Menandros. The complete entry reads, "Menander: a comic poet of the New Comedy, *strabos*, but sharp of mind and absolutely mad about women"; translation supplied by Gordon M. Kirkwood.

13. Letter to the writer, 18 April 1989. Bernard Ashmole, in his publication of this bust, notes that, since it is the only one crafted with incised pupils, it "contrives to convey the impression that the poet squinted as Suidas says he did" ("Menander: An Inscribed Bust," *American Journal of Archaeology* 77 [1973]: 61).

14. Richter, *Portraits*, 2:234.

12

VALIDATION (AND DISCOVERY) BY EXPERIMENT

Producing a Three-Actor *Ion*

In January 1997, I staged a production of *Ion* for the Lubbock (Texas) Community Theatre, giving me the opportunity to test whether Euripides' "tragedy," as it was classified in the fifth century, would take the stage in modern times as a "romantic comedy." A secondary aim was to see whether a double-purchase pulley system would prevent a flying actor from revolving uncontrollably. However, as work progressed, a third question emerged: would the show play more effectively if the cast was limited to only three actors?

Performances confirmed the validity of both initial hypotheses: audiences were charmed and amused by this adaptation of Euripides' ironic, tongue-in-cheek fairy tale; and Hermes was able to descend from the upper level secure in the knowledge that his front and not his backside would be presented to the audience. In the course of planning, casting, rehearsals, and performance, many small discoveries about the original intentions of the playwright came to light, but one major and one minor revelation emerged: Euripides included more minor roles than the plot required, apparently to fit the abilities of a talented Third Actor; and the playwright concocted a new legend involving Athena's slaying of a hitherto unknown Gorgon to add suspense and comic confusion to an otherwise straightforward poison plot.

MISREADING ARISTOTLE

Aristotle is inadvertently responsible for the Western world's assumption that tragedy concerns only plays involving the unhappy endings of kings and attendant royalty. This misinterpretation results from elevating what Aristotle clearly states is his personal preference for unhappy endings into an absolute requirement of tragedy. Although he writes that in his "Perfect Plot, . . . the hero's fortunes must not be from misery to happiness, but on the contrary from happiness to misery,"[1] this represents his ideal, not a statement of what he saw taking place on the Athenian stage. In a different passage, concerning time limits for tragedy, he acknowledges the existence of happy-ending plays, writing that tragedies must be of "a length which allows of the hero passing by a series of probable and necessary stages *from misfortune to happiness*, or from happiness to misfortune" (emphasis added).[2] Just as Neoclassic commentators transformed Aristotle's preferences for a single plot line and near-continuous stage time into two of the sacrosanct "Three Unities," later ages have transmogrified his predilection for unhappy endings into a *sine qua non*. Since the Renaissance, tragedy has meant a play with an unhappy ending; in the present age, the term has been expanded to encompass any tearful occasion: "TRAGEDY IN NEW MEXICO!! SCHOOL BUS STRIKES BRIDGE ABUTMENT," scream today's headlines.[3] However, for the fifth-century Greeks who attended the theatre, "happy tragedy" was not oxymoronic, and "unhappy tragedy" would not have been redundant.

TRAGEDY: THE CATCHALL CATEGORY

Comedy, for the Greeks, was narrowly defined: the time (at least in our few examples) is the present, the situation is current, and the characters are either living persons or recognizable types taken from the streets of Athens and its environs. The gods, when present, were not very godlike. The category was broad enough to include fantasies woven around current affairs, plays like *The Frogs* and *The Birds*. The satyr play, in similar fashion, had specific requirements: the plot was a broad travesty on the mythic affairs of gods and folkloric figures, and the chorus was always composed of those libidinous half-man, half-animal creatures known as satyrs. Frequently, a drunken god or demigod, often Herakles, was woven into the low comedy plot.

Neither comedy nor satyr play allowed room for happy-ending tales of the long-ago-and-far-away, stories that today would be classified as "romantic comedy"; for the Greeks, such plays were lumped in with the tragedies. As Bernard Knox points out, tragedy was a broad category encompassing everything that did not fall within the narrow definitions of comedy or satyr play.[4] (Euripides was allowed, in one instance, to substitute *Alkestis*, a romantic comedy, for the usual satyr play.)

The surviving plays confirm that Athenians did not expect all tragedies to end sadly. Although eighteen of the thirty-one recognized tragedies (*Alkestis* is not included here) have unhappy conclusions, there are at least nine that end with the protagonists better off at the end than they were at the beginning: *Eumenides*, *Elektra* (Sophocles), *Philoktetes*, *Oedipus at Colonus*, *Herakleidae*, *Iphigenia in Tauris*, *Ion*, *Helen* — and even *Orestes*, where the last-minute intervention of Apollo brings happy if improbable solutions to its many problems.

Four other tragedies have quasi-happy endings. It is true that *The Persians* bemoan their defeat in tragic fashion, but this play was performed only eight years after these same Persians had robbed, raped, and pillaged their way across the Greek countryside; if a play titled *The Iraqis* were presented today, an American audience would be unlikely to shed sympathetic tears as Saddam Hussein agonized over news of his army's defeat. In *Andromache*, the heroine is rescued from her plight, but vanishes midway through the play, making it difficult to determine whose change of fortune one is supposed to follow. Euripides' *Elektra* may be unhappy about her forthcoming exile, but she is happy that her enemies have been slain, that she has found a suitable husband, and that her brother has been set on a clear pathway to expiation for his matricide. *Iphigenia at Aulis* ends unhappily if the heroine dies upon the altar of Artemis; in the more likely happy ending, the goddess intercedes just as the sacrificial knife is poised to descend.

Overall, at least 29 percent of the tragedies have definitely happy endings; if the four plays of uncertain — but probably happy — outcome are added to this list, the percentage reaches 42 percent. Bear in mind, too, that the preserved plays were mostly chosen by "dramateurs" like Aristotle, who preferred unhappy endings. But even so, considering only scripts in hand, the percentage of happy endings is sufficiently large to demonstrate that the Greeks were not totally devoted to gloom and doom in their tragedies.

EURIPIDES AND COMEDY

Many of Euripides' plays have comic elements. Iolaus, in *The Herakleidae*, is a doddering old man clad in battered, antique armor purloined from a temple wall; he is so senile that he must be led into battle by an attendant. In *Iphigenia in Tauris*, Orestes and his sister have a comic recognition scene; *Orestes*, after a dankly naturalistic opening, proceeds to a comic confrontation between Orestes and Menelaus over the hapless Hermione; Knox finds comedy in the mock-tragic scenes at the beginning of *Elektra*;[5] Menelaus, in *The Trojan Women*, can best be played as a pompous buffoon.

The lost *Alexander* (an honorific for Paris) should be mentioned in a discussion of Euripides' comedies. Working from fragments, Ruth Scodel has been able to reconstruct the plot outline of this play, which was part of a tetralogy that included *The Trojan Women*.[6] According to her reading, Alexander-Paris, having been abandoned by Queen Hekuba as an infant, was found and reared by a shepherd. Grown to manhood but unaware of his true parentage, he comes to Troy as a competitor in the games, seeking to pit his athletic abilities against those of the children of Priam. Hekuba, seeing a strong physical resemblance between the young shepherd and her husband, concludes that he is Priam's bastard, one who might supplant her own children in their father's affections. She may also fear that this stranger is likely to defeat her sons in the forthcoming athletic contests. At any rate, Hekuba resolves to kill the unknown youth; but just as Alexander's life is about to end, his true parentage is revealed. Mother and son are joyfully united, and a god, probably Aphrodite, appears to provide a suitable coda for this tale of a discarded child and a murder-bent mother.

The parallels with *Ion* are striking. In both, a noble child is left to die and a wife bitterly resents her husband's supposed bastard; she hatches a murder plot, and a last-minute revelation is followed by a joyful reunion — with the blessing of a goddess. Scodel does not mention the similarities, but if *Ion* is a comedy in contemporary terms, *Alexander* must also be a comedy.

ION

The plot of *Ion* is typical of romantic comedy. Set before the temple of Apollo at Delfi, a lengthy prologue is delivered by a very un-godlike Hermes (the Third Actor). He tells how Creusa, then a young maiden, had an affair with Apollo. She gave birth, and Apollo instructed her to abandon their son in a cave. The child apparently vanished; Hermes, at Apollo's bidding, has brought the baby to Delfi, where he is adopted by the Oracle. Now, some years later, a childless Creusa and her husband, Xuthus, the present king of Athens, are coming to Delfi hoping that Apollo will grant them an end to their childlessness.

Hermes departs, and Ion, the lost child now grown to young manhood, is introduced. He is a slave, a foundling whose days are devoted to supervising the women who decorate the various altars, sweeping the porch of Apollo's shrine, and chasing away the many birds which delight in nesting in the temple columns and defecating on the sacred precincts. He sings an ode to his broom, made from the branches of Apollo's sacred laurel. His life, he tells us, is rich and satisfying; he cannot imagine a finer existence than one spent in service to the Sun God.

Enter the chorus, a group of tourists enchanted by the beauty and grandeur of Delfi. They rush hither and yon, exclaiming on each newly discovered marvel. These women, Ion learns, are the household slaves of Xuthus and Creusa.

Enter their mistress, a woman of noble bearing, who sits surrounded by her attendants, tears streaming down her face (fig. 70). "What is the matter?" Ion enquires, and she replies, "Nothing, only the memory of a long-ago happening, summoned up by the sight of Apollo's temple; it is a woman's problem and therefore of no consequence."

Creusa, queen of Athens, is married to a foreigner from Achaea, a warrior who saved the city from threatened invasion. Ion, having learned that she and her husband have come to Delfi hoping that Apollo will grant them a child, explains his own status as slave and foundling; the two establish an immediate rapport. Creusa then recounts a fanciful tale of "her friend" who was seduced by Apollo and then abandoned by him: Ion's simple faith in the Sun God is shaken by this tale.

Xuthus (Third Actor) arrives and enters the temple to consult the Pythian Oracle. He returns shortly afterward to chase Ion around the stage in what appears to be a homosexual pursuit (fig. 71). Ion threatens to shoot Xuthus with the bow and arrow he keeps to drive off offending birds. Xuthus then reveals that Apollo's Oracle has prophesied that the first person he meets on leaving the temple will be his true son. The two speculate on how this might have come about and conclude that Xuthus, on a youthful trip to Delfi, fathered Ion with the assistance of a pretty temple girl.

After some hesitation, Ion agrees to go to Athens — but as a casual visitor; his relationship to Xuthus is to be concealed from Creusa, who would be insanely jealous if she discovered that her husband had been given a son while she remained childless. Xuthus insists that, before leaving Delfi, they arrange a celebratory feast. The members of the chorus, who have overheard everything, are threatened with death if they reveal Ion's true identity to the Queen.

Father and newfound son depart, the chorus takes the stage to express

FIGURE 70. *Queen Creusa among her attendants.*

FIGURE 71. *King Xuthus embraces Ion.*

foreboding about the awful things in store. Creusa enters leading a dotty old man (Third Actor); he is a household slave, who has long been her teacher and confidant. Unable to keep the secret, the chorus blurts out all the happenings to the queen, who bitterly resents Xuthus' affection for his new-found son; she is also furious with Apollo for rewarding her husband and ignoring her plight. She decides to kill Ion with a drop of Gorgon's blood, sending the old man to slip the poison into Ion's wine cup during the feast.

The chorus then delivers what amounts to a comic *parabasis*, haranguing the audience about the virtue of women and the perfidy of men. A servant (Third Actor) arrives seeking the queen, who is in hiding until the murder is completed. The servant explains that the poison plot was discovered when a dove, drinking from Ion's wine portion, fell dead. After extracting details of the poison plot from the Old Man, Ion has begun a search for Creusa, planning to take immediate vengeance. The servant departs, sent in a wrong direction by the chorus, and a distraught, disheveled queen rushes onstage, now aware of her great danger. The chorus assists her onto the small altar, knowing that its hallowed precincts will offer protection from assault. (As mentioned earlier, the altar-as-sanctuary became a standard plot device of later Roman comedy.)

Ion arrives in an agitated state, sword in one hand and dead bird in the other (fig. 72). He is determined to kill this treacherous woman, but does not dare violate the sanctity of Apollo's altar. As they reach a stand-off, the Oracle (Third Actor) enters from the temple, carrying a dusty old cradle. She explains that Ion first came to Delfi in this cradle and that she has kept it hidden all these years. She advises Ion to begin a search for his mother, starting here in Delfi.

As the Oracle departs, Creusa recognizes the cradle as the one in which she abandoned her baby — much as Miss Prism in *The Importance of Being Earnest* recognizes the baby-laden handbag she absentmindedly left at the cloakroom of Victoria Station. Creusa is able to describe the baby clothing and trinkets contained in the cradle, convincing Ion that she is indeed his mother; they embrace in glorious reunion.

As they attempt to puzzle out how all of this came about, Athena (again, the Third Actor) enters from above to tie up the loose ends of the plot, explaining that she has been asked by Apollo to speak for him because he is too embarrassed to make an appearance. The goddess affirms that Creusa is truly Ion's mother, and Apollo his real father. Xuthus' supposed paternity, Athena explains, was just a little fib that Apollo invented to keep everyone happy. Creusa is instructed to take her son to Athens, where he will eventually ascend the throne and become the eponymous father of the Greek

FIGURE 72. *Ion threatens Creusa as she cowers on the altar.*

people. Xuthus is to go on believing that Ion is his son, and he is to learn nothing of Creusa's youthful fling with Apollo.

Athena swears the chorus to secrecy (fig. 73), and this time the women of the chorus will hold their tongues. Creusa forgives Apollo his transgressions, and Ion, although still mystified by the many twists and turns of the plot, is content that he has at last found his mother. Creusa and her son depart for Athens, with the goddess providing protection on their journey. The chorus quits the stage with a final wry endorsement of the gods' superior wisdom and judgment.

From the bare bones of the plot, it is obvious that this is not a serious tragedy, but rather a fanciful story about all-too-human gods and mythic figures. Hermes describes himself as "messenger boy for the gods." Ion is a *naïf* suddenly thrust into a world beyond his comprehension. Creusa is a comic-melodramatic figure caught somewhere between genuine tears and an overacted stage grief; Xuthus lacks the aura of a warrior-hero; instead, he is a pleasant, complacent husband who lives happily with his less-than-immaculate wife. The Old Man is clearly senile, and the Servant might be an ancestor of the Roman Running Slave. Apollo's Oracle, after her years of prophesying, is more than a little cynical about her divine pronouncements. Athena's opening line is a very ungodlike, "No, wait a minute!"

The rulers of the heavens are shallow creatures, guiding human destinies

FIGURE 73. *The chorus swears to be silent.*

in a haphazard manner. Euripides takes delight in pointing out Apollo's clumsy manipulation of events: Ion nearly kills both his supposed father and his real mother. Gilbert Murray quite accurately calls *Ion* "the most ironic of the extant plays, and perhaps the most blasphemous."[7] Interestingly, Texas audiences did not regard Euripides' ridicule of the gods as an attack on religion in general.

The human characters are those of high comedy, people preoccupied with everyday concerns and human relationships. Xuthus and Creusa may be king and queen of Athens, but their actions are those of a middle-aged married couple on a trip out of town. "Have you been worried, my dear, that I was so late arriving?" Xuthus asks his queen. This is not the level of concern one expects from the lofty figures of serious tragedy; imagine Oedipus greeting Jocasta with "Well, dear, did you have a nice nap?"

The Mise-en-Scène

The setting requirements for the play are simple: offstage entrances, a door into the interior of Apollo's temple, murals for the chorus to gawk at, and a small altar. The scene designer chose to adapt a *naiskos* from the vase paintings and to cover the walls with cartoonish murals. Found space presented limitations; a steel pipe supporting the roof of the building stood in the middle of the stage, so the *naiskos* was positioned to allow the pipe to became the upstage column supporting the roof of the *naiskos*.

The costumes were based upon Greek attire, but with brighter, more varied hues than ancient costumers could have obtained with their limited supply of natural dyes. The garments were cut to allow the freedom of movement appropriate to comedy. Makeup substituted for masks, with women's parts played by women — except for the two female roles necessarily assigned to the Third Actor. (An experimental performance using masks and an all-male cast must wait for another day.) The properties were items of everyday life: a bow and arrows, garlands, a broom, laurel branches, a bracelet, a sword, cups, a water pitcher, and a stuffed bird.

THE THIRD ACTOR

In the very earliest planning, no thought was given to the possibility of presenting the play with only three actors: testing the validity of *Ion*-as-comedy seemed a sufficient problem — and, after all, a valid experiment should avoid too many unknowns. However, further study of the play's structure made limiting the cast to only three actors seem almost a necessity.

Ion and Creusa are both straightforward continuing roles, played by the protagonist and deuteragonist; the Third Actor parts (Hermes, Xuthus, Old Man, Servant, Oracle, and Athena) all have brief appearances and are never seen again. It would be difficult to find six competent actors willing to commit to a lengthy rehearsal period for the dubious rewards of brief appearances in small parts. But the six roles combined would provide an almost irresistible challenge for a seasoned actor, and such sextupling would have a strong audience appeal.

A question then arose: why had Euripides put together this series of non-integrated appearances by the Third Actor? Why does each character vanish almost as soon as he or she becomes familiar to the audience? Why would a master playwright create six briefly seen characters when three or four would have sufficed?

At first, this succession of minor roles made little sense; Gilbert Murray, whose grasp of dramatic structure was apparently stronger than his memory, "improved" the composition of the plot by mistakenly giving Hermes a concluding reappearance rather than allowing Athena to appear as yet another character.[8]

There is an obvious explanation for these questions, one lying in the area of performance, not literary composition. Since the transmutable actor has always been a crowd-pleaser, these six parts were surely put together to suit the talents of a popular, versatile Third Actor with a gift for comedy.

Classical audiences were well acquainted with the three-actor convention of tragedy and would have had little difficulty in figuring out which actor was playing a particular role or series of roles. Of course, placing such emphasis upon the lowly Third Actor was most unusual; Demosthenes sneered at one Third Actor because he "played small parts to their [Actors One and Two] leads, picking up figs and grapes and olives."[9] Possibly the elevation of the Third Actor to a starring role was some kind of inside joke between the playwright and his audience.

"THE VESSEL WITH THE PESTLE"

Euripides showed little hesitation in embroidering mythologies to suit his dramatic purposes. For *Iphigenia at Aulis*, the playwright illustrated Clytemnestra's loyalty and Agamemnon's brutality by inventing an earlier family for Clytemnestra, one ruthlessly slain by her future husband. In the lost *Melanippe Sophe*, he made Xuthus the biological father of Ion, while in the present play Apollo was given that honor.

In *Ion*, Euripides endows the poison potion with a certain historical authenticity by creating a previously unknown Gorgon for Athena to slay. The playwright then lets the goddess extract both a *killing* and a *healing* drop of blood from the slain creature. In Euripides' version, vials of these two potions are both permanently affixed to a bracelet which has been passed down until it now hangs from the wrist of Creusa. Timothy Gantz doubts a folkloric basis for this account:

> This alternative tale of the Gorgoneion on the aigis could conceivably be old, since Homer has nothing to contradict it; certainly it fits well with the Homeric notion of the Gorgon as a generic monster. On the other hand, it seems suspicious that such a duel between goddess and Gorgon never appears in art, where it would have enlivened the usual iconography. Euripides' purpose in mentioning the event is to provide a source for the poison with which Kreousa proposes to kill Ion; as that plot is likely peculiar to this play, so perhaps is the background for it.[10]

The twin vials are seemingly identical; because they are permanently attached to the bracelet, Creusa is forced to give both healing and killing potions to a senile, half-blind old man, hoping he will have wit and vision enough to put the killing rather than the healing drop into Ion's wine cup. The inevitable confusion which follows not only has the effect of building suspense, but also offers opportunities for comic business: possibly Queen and Old Man puzzle over which capsule is which; they agree, and then disagree; after several changes are rung on this theme, the Old Man exits in a state of total confusion, holding the vials quizzically before his age-dimmed eyes. The situation is very like Danny Kaye's comic perplexity in *The Court Jester*, where "the vessel with the pestle has the pellet with the poison." In this film, confusion is played effectively through seemingly endless variations.

Although no words in the script spell out this pantomimic business, there may have been related lines that were omitted by some long-ago copyist as inconsequential. Euripides had some dramatic purpose for inventing this complicated legend of the Gorgon's blood, and it would likely have been a comic one.

FLYING WITH THE DOUBLE-PURCHASE PULLEY SYSTEM

Greek engineers were well aware of the mechanical advantage gained from pulley systems; without them, the Parthenon could not have been built. The very simple arrangement (fig. 74) used to "fly" Hermes at the opening of *Ion* is well within fifth-century technical understanding. Use of this double-purchase pulley solved the problem of the revolving deity: hung from two slightly separated points of suspension, Hermes was able to make his flight facing the audience. One minor difficulty arose; when the actor unhooked himself, the two lines had a tendency to twist together, making the empty pulley difficult to raise.

Braided rather than twisted rope might have reduced this problem, but such speculation must be made on almost no evidence: although the artisan rope-maker was very much in demand during Greek and Roman times, little is known about this craft. We do know that hemp and papyrus were the chief raw materials, but information about manufacturing methods is sadly lacking.[11] For specialized theatrical use, thinner ropes might have been made of horsehair or leather, using techniques similar to those employed by Mexican and American cowboys — and perhaps the fabled horsemen of Thessaly.

FIGURE 74. *Hermes alights from his flight.*

CONCLUSION

Four additions to present knowledge have emerged from this production: (1) *Ion* plays well as a witty, ironic, romantic comedy similar in genre to Shakespeare's *The Winter's Tale*, which also has a plot centering around the finding of a lost child; (2) Euripides enjoyed the services of a talented Third Actor, and he utilized that actor's talents to create a comic reversal of high and low in the usual acting hierarchy; (3) the twin vials of Gorgon's blood were invented by Euripides to add comic business and a *soupçon* of suspense to the projected poisoning of the play's protagonist; (4) a double-hung pulley system allows a flying actor to maintain orientation.

The stage is seldom utilized as a laboratory to test historical suppositions. This is unfortunate, for even with its many shortcomings as a means of experimentation, valid discoveries can emerge from the requirements of production and performance.

NOTES

1. Aristotle, *Poetics*, 1453a12.

2. Ibid., 1451a12.

3. "Hybris" or "hubris" has suffered a fate similar to that of "tragedy." Newspaper, television, and radio commentators now routinely employ "hubris" as a synonym for "overweening pride," a usage that would puzzle the ancient Greeks.

4. See Bernard Knox, "Euripidean Comedy" in *Word and Action*, 350–374.

5. Ibid., 251–254.

6. Ruth Scodel, *The Trojan Trilogy of Euripides*, 20–42.

7. George Gilbert Aimé Murray, "Euripides," in *Encyclopaedia Britannica*, 14th ed.

8. Ibid.

9. Demosthenes, *De Corona*, 262.

10. Timothy Gantz, *Early Greek Myth*, 448.

11. See J. G. Landels, *Engineering in the Ancient World* (Berkeley: University of California Press, 1978), 109.

BIBLIOGRAPHY

Aeschines. *The Speeches of Aeschines*. Translated by Charles Darwin Adams. Cambridge, Mass.: Harvard University Press, 1919.

Akurgal, Ekrem. *Ancient Civilizations and Ruins of Turkey*. 6th ed. Istanbul: Haşet Kitabevi, 1985.

Andocides. *Greek Orators IV*. Edited and translated by Michael Edwards. Warminster, England: Aris & Phillips, 1995.

———. *On the Mysteries*. In *Minor Attic Orators*, vol. 1. Translated by K. J. Maidment. Cambridge, Mass.: Harvard University Press, 1953.

Andronikos, Manolis. "Anaskafi Verginas." *Praktika* (1983-A).

———. *Vergina: The Royal Tombs*. Athens: Ekdotike Athenon S.A., 1984.

Anti, Carlo. *Teatri greci arcaici da Minosse a Pericle*. Padua: le Tre Venezie, 1947.

Anti, Carlo, and Luigi Polacco. *Nuove ricerche sui teatri greci arcaici*. Padua: Edizioni Cedam, 1969.

Aristotle. *Aristotle on the Art of Poetry*. Translated and edited by Ingram Bywater. New York: Garland Publishing, 1980.

———. *Problems*. 2 vols. Translated by W. S. Hett. Cambridge, Mass.: Harvard University Press, 1953.

Ashby, Clifford. "The Case for the Rectangular/Trapezoidal Orchestra." *Theatre Research International* 13 (Spring 1988): 1–20.

———. "The Playwright and the 'Dramateur.'" *Dramatists Guild Quarterly* (Winter 1998): 14–20.

———. "The 'Theatre' Altar at Corinth." *Theatre Southwest* 13 (May 1986): 28.

Ashmole, Bernard. "Menander: An Inscribed Bust." *American Journal of Archaeology* 77 (1973): 61.

Athenaeus. *The Deipnosophists*. Translated by Charles Burton Gulick. 7 vols. Cambridge, Mass.: Harvard University Press, 1951.

Barish, Jonas. *The Anti-theatrical Prejudice*. Berkeley: University of California Press, 1981.

Bean, George E. *Aegean Turkey: An Archaeological Guide*. 2nd impression corrected. London: Benn, 1967.

Bethe, Erich. *Prolegomena zur Geschichte des Theaters im Altertum*. Leipzig: Von S. Hirzel, 1896.

———. "Der Spielplatz des Aischylos." *Hermes* 59 (1924): 108–117.

———. "Thymeliker und Skeniker." *Hermes* 36 (1901): 597–601.

Bieber, Margarete. *Die Denkmäler zum Theaterwesen im Altertum*. Berlin: Vereinigung wissenschaftlicher Verleger, 1920.

———. *Griechische Kleidung*. Berlin: Walter de Gruyter & Co., 1928.

———. *The History of the Greek and Roman Theatre*. 2nd ed. revised and enlarged. Princeton: Princeton University Press, 1961.

———. Review of *Teatri greci arcaici*. *American Journal of Philology* 53 (1949): 449–450.

———. Review of *Teatri greci arcaici*. *Art Bulletin* 31 (March 1949): 61–63.

Blum, G., and A. Plassart. "Orchomène d'Arcadie: Fouilles de 1913." *Bulletin de Correspondance Hellénique* 38 (1914): 71–81.

Boyd, Thomas D. "The Arch and the Vault in Greek Architecture." *American Journal of Archaeology* 82 (1978): 83–100.

Brockett, Oscar G. *History of the Theatre*. 7th ed. Boston: Allyn & Bacon, 1995.

Buck, Carl D. "Architectural Remains in Ikaria." *Papers of the American School of Classical Studies at Athens* 5 (1886–1890): 54–69.

Buckham, Philip Wentworth. *The Theatre of the Greeks*. 2nd ed. altered and much enlarged by John William Donaldson. Cambridge: W. P. Grant, 1827.

Bulle, Heinrich. *Eine Skenographie*. Berlin: Verlag von Walter de Gruyter & Co., 1934.

Bulle, Heinrich, and Heinrich Wirsing. *Szenenbilder zum Griechischen Theater des 5. Jahrhunderts v. Chr*. Berlin: im Verlage Gebr. Mann, 1950.

Bywater, Ingram. *Aristotle on the Art of Poetry*. Oxford: Clarendon Press, 1909.

Calder, W. M. "The Dithyramb — An Anatolian Dirge." *Classical Review* 36 (1922): 11–14.

Clark, Barrett H., ed. *European Theories of the Drama*. Revised ed. New York: Crown Publishers, 1947. Newly revised ed. New York: Crown Publishers, 1965.

Collart, Paul. "Le théâtre de Philippes." *Bulletin de Correspondance Hellénique* 53 (1928): 74–124.

Csapo, Eric, and William J. Slater. *The Context of Ancient Drama*. Ann Arbor: University of Michigan Press, 1995.

Demosthenes. *Against Meidias*. Edited and translated by Douglas M. MacDowell. Oxford: Clarendon Press, 1990.

———. *Against Meidias*. Translated by J. H. Vince. Cambridge, Mass.: Harvard University Press, 1935.

———. *On the Peace*. Translated by J. H. Vince. Cambridge, Mass.: Harvard University Press, 1954.

———. *Private Orations*. Translated by A. T. Murray. Cambridge, Mass.: Harvard University Press, 1936.

Diggle, James. *Euripidea*. Oxford: Clarendon Press, 1994.

Dilke, O. A. W. "Details and Chronology of Greek Theatre Caveas." *Annual of the British School at Athens* 45 (1950): 21–62.

———. "The Greek Theatre Cavea." *Annual of the British School at Athens* 43 (1948): 125–192.

Dinsmoor, William Bell. *The Architecture of Ancient Greece*. 3rd ed. revised. London: B. T. Batsford, 1950.

————. "The Athenian Theater of the Fifth Century." In *Studies Presented to David Moore Robinson*, ed. George E. Mylonas, 311–330. St. Louis: Washington University, 1972.

Dörpfeld, W. Review of "De certaminibus thymelicis," by Johannes Frei. *Deutsche Litteraturzeitung* 29 (20 July 1901): cols. 1816–1818.

————. "Thymele und Skene." *Hermes* 37 (1902): 249–257.

Dörpfeld, W., and E. Reisch. *Das Griechische Theater*. Athens: n.p. 1896; reprinted Darmstadt: Scientia Verlag Aalen, 1966.

Dubech, Lucien. *Histoire générale illustrée du théâtre*, vol. 1, *Le théâtre Grec, le théâtre Latin*. Paris: Librairie de France, 1931–1935.

Duckworth, George E., ed. *The Complete Roman Drama*. 2 vols. New York: Random House, 1942.

Ducrey, Pierre, and Olivier Picard. "Recherches à Latô IV: Le théâtre." *Bulletin de Correspondance Hellénique* 95 (1971): 515–531.

————. "Recherches à Latô V: Le prytanée." *Bulletin de Correspondance Hellénique* 96 (1972): 567–590.

Elderkin, G. W. "Two Mosaics Representing the Seven Wise Men." *American Journal of Archaeology* 29 (1935): 92–111.

Evans, Sir Arthur. *The Palace of Minos*. 4 vols. London: Macmillan and Co., 1930.

Franke, Peter Robert. "Albanian im Altertum." *Antike Welt* (1983): 11–65.

Frel, Jiri'. *Greek Portraits in the J. Paul Getty Museum*. Malibu, Calif.: Getty Museum, 1981.

Gaertringen, F. Freiherr Hiller von, ed. *Inschriften von Priene*. Berlin: Georg Reimer, 1906.

Gantz, Timothy. *Early Greek Myth*. Baltimore: Johns Hopkins University Press, 1993.

Gebhard, Elizabeth R. "The Form of the Orchestra in the Early Greek Theatre." *Hesperia* 43 (1974): 428–440.

————. *The Theatre at Isthmia*. Chicago: University of Chicago Press, 1973.

Gerkan, Armin von, and Wolfgang Müller-Wiener. *Das Theater von Epidauros*. Stuttgart: W. Kohlhammer, 1961.

Ginouvès, René. *Le théâtron à gradins droits et l'Odéon d'Argos*. Paris: Librairie Philosophique J. Vrin, 1972.

Goldhill, Simon D. Review of *Public and Performance in Greek Theatre*. *Theatre Research International* 15 (1990): 262.

Green, J. R. *Theatre in Ancient Greek Society*. London: Routledge, 1994.

Haigh, A. E. *The Attic Theatre*. Oxford: Clarendon Press, 1889.

Harlan, Jack R. *The Living Fields: Our Agricultural Heritage*. Cambridge: Cambridge University Press, 1995.

Hodge, A. Trevor. *The Woodwork of Greek Roofs*. Cambridge: Cambridge University Press, 1960.

Hughes, Alan. "Comic Stages in Magna Graecia: The Evidence of the Vases." *Theatre Research International* 21 (Summer 1996): 95–107.

Kernodle, George R. "Recent Scholarship on the Greek Theatre." *Educational Theatre Journal* 3 (1951): 129–134.

Knox, Bernard. *Word and Action: Essays on the Ancient Theater.* Baltimore: Johns Hopkins University Press, 1979.

Landels, J. G. *Engineering in the Ancient World.* Berkeley: University of Chicago Press, 1978.

Lattimore, Richmond, ed. *The Complete Greek Tragedies.* 9 vols. Chicago: University of Chicago Press, 1953–1959.

Laurenzi, Luciano. "Nuove contributi alla topografia storico-archeologico di Coo." *Historia* 5(4): 603–626.

Lefkowitz, Mary R. *The Lives of the Greek Poets.* London: Gerald Duckworth & Co., 1981.

Lendle, Otto. "Überlegungen zum Bühnenkran." In Egert Pöhlmann, *Studien zur Bühnendichtung und zum Theaterbau der Antike,* 165–172. Frankfurt am Main: Peter Lang, 1995.

Maas, Michael. Review of *Teatri greci arcaici. Gnomon* 46 (1974): 95–97.

MacDonald, William A. Review of *Teatri greci arcaici. American Journal of Archaeology* 53 (1949): 412–414.

Markman, Sidney D. Review of *Teatri greci arcaici. Classical Journal* 44 (January 1949): 278–279.

Mastronarde, Donald J. "Actors on High: The Skene Roof, the Crane, and the Gods in Attic Drama." *Classical Antiquity* 9 (October 1990): 247–294.

Mitens, Karina. *Teatri greci e teatri inspirati all'architettura Greca in Sicilia nell'Italia meriodionale c. 350–50 a.C.* Rome: "l'Erma" di Bretschneider, 1988.

Modona, Aldo Neppi. *Gli edifici teatrali greci e romani.* Florence: Leo S. Olschki Editore, 1961.

———. *L'Isola di Coo nell'antichità classica.* n.p.: Instituto Storico-Archeologia di Rodi, 1933–1941.

Moretti, J.-Ch. "Argos: Le théâtre." *Bulletin de Correspondance Hellénique* 112 (1988): 716–720.

Mussche, H. F., et al. *Thorikos, a Guide to the Excavations.* Brussels: Comité des Fouilles Belges en Grèce, 1974.

———. *Thorikos 1965: Rapport préliminaire.* Brussels: Comité des Fouilles Belges en Grèce, 1967.

Nauck, Augustus. *Euripidis Perditarum Tragoediarum Fragmenta.* Leipzig: B. G. Teubner, 1892.

Oates, Whitney J., and Eugene O'Neill, Jr., eds. *The Complete Greek Drama.* 2 vols. New York: Random House, 1938.

Page, Denys L. *Actors' Interpolations in Greek Tragedy.* New York: Garland Publishing, 1987; reprint of 1934 edition.

Petrakos, Valiseios. *Ramnous.* Athens: n.p., 1991.

Pickard-Cambridge, A. W. *Dithyramb, Tragedy, and Comedy.* 2nd ed.; revised by T. B. L. Webster. Oxford: Clarendon Press, 1962.

———. *The Dramatic Festivals of Athens.* Oxford: Oxford University Press, 1953.

———. Review of *Teatri greci arcaici*. *Classical Review* 62 (1948): 125–128.

———. *The Theatre of Dionysus in Athens*. Oxford: Oxford University Press, 1946.

Poe, Joe Park. "The Altar in the Fifth-Century Theater." *Classical Antiquity* 8 (April 1989): 116–139.

Polacco, Luigi, and Carlo Anti. *Nuove ricerche sui teatri greci*. Padua: Cedam-Casa Editrice Dott. Antonio Milani, 1969.

Polacco, Luigi, and Carlo Anti, with collaboration of Maria Trojani. *Il teatro antico de Siracusa*. 2 vols. Rimini: Maggiolo Editore, 1981.

Pollux. *Pollucis Onomasticon*. Edited by Erich Bethe. 3 vols. Stuttgart: B. G. Teubner, 1967; originally published 1900.

Pouilloux, Jean. *La Forteresse de Rhamnonte*. Paris: E. de Boccard, 1954.

Ramsay, W. M. *The Cities and Bishoprics of Phrygia*. New York: Arno Press, 1975; reprint of 1895 ed.

Rees, Kelley. *The So-Called Rule of Three Actors in the Classical Greek Drama*. Chicago: University of Chicago Press, 1908.

Rehm, Rush. *Greek Tragic Theatre*. London: Routledge, 1992.

Renier, G. J. *History: Its Purpose and Method*. London: George Allen & Unwin, 1950.

Richter, Gisela M. A. *The Portraits of the Greeks*. 3 vols. London: Phaidon Press, 1965.

Richter, Julius. *Die Vertheilung der Rollen unter die Schauspieler der Griechischen Tragödie*. Berlin: Verlag von E. H. Schroeder, 1842.

Robert, Carl. "Zur Theaterfrage." *Hermes* 32 (1897): 421–453.

Robinson, Alice M. "The Cult of Asklepius and the Theatre." *Educational Theatre Journal* 30 (December 1978): 530–542.

Schanzer, Ernest. "Thomas Platter's Observations on the Elizabethan Stage." *Notes and Queries* (November 1956): 465–467.

Scodel, Ruth. *The Trojan Trilogy of Euripides*. Göttingen: Vandenhoeck & Reprecht, 1980.

———, ed. *Theater and Society in the Classical World*. Ann Arbor: University of Michigan Press, 1993.

Scully, Vincent. *The Earth, the Temple, and the Gods*. New Haven: Yale University Press, 1962. 2nd ed., revised. New Haven: Yale University Press, 1979.

Sjoquist, Eric. "Excavations at Morgantina (Serra Orlando), 1961: Preliminary Report VI." *American Journal of Archaeology* 6(6) (1962): 135–143.

Snell, Bruno. "Zwei Töpfe mit Euripides Papyri." *Hermes* 70 (1935): 119–120.

Stainhaouer, Georgios. "Diamorphosis arkaiologikou horou Orchomenou." *Deltion* 29 (1973–1974): 301.

Stanley, Audrey Eunice. "Early Theatre Structures in Ancient Greece: A Survey of Archaeological and Literary Records from the Minoan Period to 388 B.C." Ph.D. dissertation, University of California at Berkeley, 1970.

Sturzebecker, Russell L. *Athletic-Cultural Archaeological Sites in the Greco-Roman World*. Westchester, Pa.: by the author, 1985.

Suidas. *Suidae Lexicon*. Edited by Ada Adler. Stuttgart: B. G. Teubner, 1971; originally published 1928.

Taplin, Oliver. *Comic Angels*. Oxford: Clarendon Press, 1993.

————. *Greek Tragedy in Action*. London: Methuen & Co., 1978.

————. *The Stagecraft of Aeschylus*. Oxford: Oxford University Press, 1984.

Travlos, John (Ioannes N. Traulos). *Bildlexicon zur Topographie des antiken Attika*. Tübingen: Ernst Wasmuth Verlag, 1988.

————. *Pictorial Dictionary of Ancient Athens*. New York: Praeger Publishers, 1971.

Trendall, A. D., and T. B. L. Webster. *Illustrations of Greek Drama*. London: Phaidon Press, 1971.

Tzahou-Alexandri, Olga. "Anaskafi theatrou stois Trachones Attikis." *Praktika* (1980): 64–67.

Verhoogen, V. Review of *Teatri greci arcaici*. *Revue Belge de Philologie et d'Histoire* 49 (1971): 222–224.

Vince, Ronald W. *Ancient and Medieval Theatre: A Historiographical Handbook*. Westport, Conn.: Greenwood Press, 1984.

Vitruvius. *Vitruvius on Architecture*. Edited and translated by Frank Granger. 2 vols. Cambridge, Mass.: Harvard University Press, 1955–1956; originally published 1934.

Webster, T. B. L. *Greek Theatre Production*. London: Methuen & Co., 1956. 2nd ed. London: Methuen & Co., 1970.

————. *Monuments Illustrating New Comedy*. 3rd ed.; revised and enlarged by J. R. Green and A. Seeberg. 2 vols. London: Institute of Classical Studies, 1995.

Wiles, David. *Tragedy in Athens*. Cambridge: Cambridge University Press, 1997.

Winkler, John J., and Froma I. Zeitlin, eds. *Nothing to Do with Dionysos?* Princeton: Princeton University Press, 1990.

Xenophon. *Cyropaedia*. Translated by Walter Miller. 2 vols. Cambridge, Mass.: Harvard University Press, 1914.

————. *Oeconomicus*. Translated by E. C. Marchant. London: William Heinemann, 1938.

Zuntz, G. *An Inquiry into the Transmission of the Plays of Euripides*. Cambridge: Cambridge University Press, 1965.

INDEX

Acting as a profession, 111–113

Actors: cast size, 128–130, 138 n. 8, 165, 175–176; children, 134; gender, 134; interpolations, 14 n. 15; physical size, 18, 134; vocal range, 131, 133–134, 137, 153

Aeschines, 10, 122, 124–125, 130

Aeschylus, 2, 3, 17, 26, 68, 112, 122, 128, 129–130, 136; *Agamemnon*, 7, 44, 45, 63, 70, 89, 92, 101, 120, 122, 125, 129, 132, 141, 176; *Choephori*, 132, 133, 136; *Eumenides*, 46, 70, 121, 132, 167; *Oresteia*, 70, 120, 131, 132–133; *Persians*, 2, 129, 143, 167; *Prometheus Bound*, 81, 121, 129; *Proteus*, 132; *Seven against Thebes*, 129; *Suppliants*, 121, 129; *Women of Aetna*, 117 n. 25

Afterpiece, 6, 13–14 n. 14

Agathon, 7, 9, 91, 112

Agyieus, 45–46

Akurgal, Ekrem, 60 n. 23

Alexander, Margaret, 164 n. 8

Alkibiades, 65

Altar, xv, 4, 7, 91, 95, 167, 169, 172; architectural evidence, 47–59; artistic evidence, 46–47; literary evidence, 45–46; location, 25, 32, 42 ff., 59–60 n. 7; origins of the concept, 42–44

Amphiktyonic Council, 112

Anavysos *chous*, 111

Ancients' Club, 1, 8, 12–13, 42, 101

Andokides, 57, 65, 79 n. 7

Andronikos, Manolis, 48

Anthesteria, 2, 111

Anti, Carlo, 26–28

Antioch, 150, 164 n. 6

Archaeological remains, 15–17

Archelaus, 112

Aristophanes, 5, 7, 17, 26, 37, 45, 75, 81, 89, 112, 121; *Acharnians*, 8, 81, 90; *Birds*, 5, 7, 81, 90, 166; *Clouds*, 7, 81, 89, 121; *Frogs*, 37, 166; *Knights*, 5; *Lysistrata*, 121; *Peace*, 7, 81; *Thesmaphoriazusae*, 7, 75; *Wasps*, 8, 89, 121

Aristotle, 4, 8, 14 n. 21, 42, 112, 128, 145; happy and unhappy endings in tragedy, 166–167; misreading his writings, 166; number of actors, 6, 128; play length, 122–123, 129; spectacle, 9–10, 119

Arnott, Peter, xviii

Artistic remains, 17–20

Artists of Dionysos, 112–113

Assignment of roles, 138 n. 8

Athenaeus, 12, 126 n. 2

Athens, classical sites, 36–39

Attica, 35–36

Azimuth, 108–110

Barish, Jonas, 9

Bean, George, 101

Bieber, Margarete, 17–18, 27, 37–38, 47, 57, 82, 88, 139–145

Brockett, Oscar G., 40, 147

Buckham, Philip Wentworth, 42–43

Bulle, Heinrich, xviii, 66–67, 75, 82–83

Calder, W. M., 68–70

Campus Martius, 142

Charon's steps, 11
Classical sites, Athens, 36–39
Classic and Helenistic theatres, a
    comparison, 139–145
Cole, Susan Goettel, 116 n. 17
Comedies, 2, 5, 7–8, 12, 19–20, 37–38,
    64, 77, 81, 89, 121, 124, 130, 134, 165, 166,
    167–174, 175, 176–177, 179
Comic vases, 19, 47, 56, 74–75
Conductivity of materials, 116 n. 16
Csapo, Eric, 126 n. 2
Cult theatres, xiv, 55, 105, 115 n. 10

Dawn performances, 105, 109, 118–126
Demosthenes, 10, 63–65, 68, 69, 113,
    123–125, 130, 137 n. 6, 176
Didaskalia, 2, 20–22
Diggle, James, 2
Dilke, O. A. W., 25, 35, 37, 41 n. 28
Dinsmoor, William Bell, 38–39, 75–76, 97
Dionysia, City (Great), 2, 3, 6, 13 n. 4, 21,
    42, 57, 63–64, 108, 110–111, 113, 118–119,
    121–123, 124, 125–126, 145
Dionysos, 42, 45, 48, 49, 50, 57, 68–69, 122,
    123, 125, 141
Dithyramb, 10, 42, 63–66, 68–69, 78, 79
    n. 5, 111, 119
Dokos, 96 n. 11
Doorstones, 69, 79 n. 13
Dörpfeld, Wilhelm, 39, 43, 44, 57, 59–60
    n. 7, 145
"Dramateur," 8, 11, 14 n. 18, 167
Dubech, Lucien, 147

Eighth-century Greek sites, 30
Ekkyklema, 7, 70, 90–92
Elderkin, G. W., 164 n. 7
Eleos, 45
Epicharmus, 13 n. 2
Epigraphic evidence, 20–22
Euripides, 3, 4–5, 7, 9, 17, 26, 47, 68, 81,
    89–90, 112, 120, 121, 122, 134, 135, 137,
    165–179; *Alexander*, 168; *Alkestis*, 13 n. 13,
    91–92, 122, 134, 167; *Andromada*, 120;
    Bacchae, 4; *Cyclops*, 4, 132, 134; *Elektra*, 4,
    7, 121, 129, 132, 133, 167, 168; *Hekuba*, 4, 5,
    131; *Helen*, 4, 167; *Herakleidae*, 5, 46, 134,
    167–168; *Herakles*, 4, 13 n. 13, 131;
    Hippolytus, 131, 133; *Ino*, 13 n. 6; *Ion*, 4, 6,
    45, 120–121, 130, 131, 165–179; *Iphigenia at
    Aulis*, 4, 134, 167, 176; *Iphigenia in Tauris*,
    5, 46–47, 66–67, 68, 167, 168; *Medea*, 3,
    7, 87–88, 101, 131, 134; *Melanippe Sophe*,
    176; *Oineus*, 47; *Orestes*, 4, 89–90, 131,
    167, 168; *Rhesus*, 70, 120, 130, 135, 136;
    Sthenoboia, 81; *Suppliant Women*, 4, 134–
    135; *Thersites*, 4; *Theseus*, 13 n. 6;
    Thyestes, 13 n. 6; *Trojan Women*, 121, 131,
    134, 168; *Women of Trachis*, 133–134
Evans, Arthur, 25, 30

Festivals in Athens, 2, 5, 57, 59, 63–64, 111,
    112–113, 119, 128, 139
Fiechter, E., 38
Fontaine, Jean de la, 93–94
Found space, 62–63, 67, 78, 89, 95, 174
Franke, Peter Robert, 53
Furttenbach, Joseph, 93

Gantz, Timothy, 176
Garvie, A. F., 133
Gerkan, Armin von, 48, 97
Goldhill, Simon, xviii
Gould, John, 124
Greek Islands, 35, 102, 106
Green, J. R. (Richard), 8–9, 144, 147

Haigh, A. E., 43, 123
Hanson, John Arthur, 142
Healing shrines and rituals, 56, 145;
    performance at, 116–117 n. 24
Hesychius, 44
Hughes, Alan, 23 n. 3, 26, 47
Hybris (hubris), 124, 179 n. 3

Insulation materials, 108, 116 n. 16

Johnson, Samuel, 10
Jones, Frances F., 164 n. 6

Jones, Henry Arthur, 8
Jonson, Ben, 85

Karchesion, 84
Kaye, Danny, 177
Klepsydra, 60 n. 24, 122, 129
Knox, Bernard, 129–130, 167, 168

Landels, J. G., 84
Lattimore, Richmond, 4, 135, 136
Laurenzi, Luciano, 61 n. 28
Lefkowitz, Mary R., 5, 12,
Lenaia, 2, 111, 124; lighting, 116 n. 20
Lendle, Otto, 84–85, 88
Lesbos, 106, 159
Lewis, D. M., 124
Lighting the performers, 108, 109–110, 113–114, 118
Lord Mayor of London, 111
Louvre krater, 66–74

MacDonald, William A., 27, 37
Magna Graecia sites, 18, 34–35, 47, 68, 70, 89, 102, 106
Markman, Sidney D., 40
Mastronarde, Donald J., 83–84, 85, 88
Mechane, 81–87, 90, 94
Medias, 64, 68, 69, 123–124
Miller, Walter, 39
Minoan-Mycenean performance areas, 28
Mount Tamalpais, 100–101
Müller-Weiner, Wolfgang, 48, 97
Murals, 17
Murray, Gilbert, 174, 175
Mussche, H. F., 60 n. 21

Naiskos, 19, 73–74
Neoptolemus, 113
Neppi Modona, Aldo, 95 n. 9
North African sites, 35, 143

Olivier, Laurence, 6, 133
O'Neill, Eugene, Jr., 5
Onnagata (Kabuki), 134
Orchestra, 7, 11, 24–40, 42–59, 63, 65–66, 81, 83, 89, 100, 106, 109, 135, 140–144

Orientation of theatres: Anatolia, 106; the Islands, 106; Magna Graecia, 106; the Mainland, 105–106

Page, Denys L., 14 n. 15
Paraskenia, 19, 45, 64, 66–69, 71, 72, 75, 79 n. 11, 91
Parian Stone (*Marmor Parium*), 20–21, 63, 79 n. 1
Payers and players, 109
Peisistratus, 21, 63
Performance: beginning time, 116 n. 19, 118–126; time limitation, 121–123
Periaktoi, 92–93, 95
Pherecrates, 119
Philochorus, 119–120, 125–126
Phlyakes, 19, 74
Pickard-Cambridge, Arthur, 27, 37, 39, 43, 64, 67, 70, 90–91, 118–119, 121, 123–124, 130, 133, 135, 136, 145, 147
Pinakes, 22, 77, 79, 95
Plato, 9, 81, 112
Platter, Thomas, 13 n. 14
Plautus, 121; *The Merchant*, 121
Plays, extant, 3–6
Playscripts, 2–3
Poe, Joe Park, 46
Polacco, Luigi, 27–28
Pollux, 10–12, 25, 45, 46, 56, 70, 71, 78, 90, 92, 95, 96 n. 12, 145
Porter, John R., 116 n. 19
Pratinas, 44
Proskenion, 48, 70, 75–77, 80 n. 28, 88, 89, 95

Rainouts, 16 n. 20
Ramps, 87–88, 95 n. 9
Ramsay, W. M., 79 n. 13
Rehm, Rush, 21, 92
Reisch, E., 43–44, 57
Renier, G. J., 145
Richter, Gisella M. A., 147–148, 149, 152, 162
Richter, Julius, 129
Robinson, Alice M., 56
Robinson, Henry S., 55

Role distribution, 129–137, 153, 165, 175

Roofs, 18, 71, 75, 76, 80 n. 25, 87, 89–90, 91, 95, 96 n. 11; flat roof, 75, 87–89; roof tiles, 22, 75, 89

"Royal" door, 69–74

Rural Dionysia, 2, 111, 124

Satyr plays, 2, 4, 6, 7, 122, 123, 125, 128, 130, 132, 136, 139, 166–167

Schanzer, Ernest, 13–14 n. 14

Scholiast, 12, 90

Scodel, Ruth, 168

Scott, Alwyn P., 99

Scully, Vincent, 97–99, 100, 101

Seated Menanders, 147–162

Slater, William J., 1, 75, 112

Snell, Bruno, 4

Snodgrass, Anthony, 40

Socrates, 7, 9, 81, 124–125

Solar heating, 108

Sophilos, 30

Sophocles, 3, 17, 26, 45–46, 68, 120, 122, 128, 135, 136, 139, 154; *Antigone*, 120, 131, 136; *Elektra*, 120, 167; *Oedipus at Colonus*, 70, 131, 135–136, 167; *Oedipus the King*, 6, 76, 131, 133, 134, 139, 174

Spectacle, 9–10, 63, 65, 85, 119, 145

Spring weather, Athens, 116 n. 19

Stage as laboratory, 114–115, 179

Stäis, B., 39

Stanley, Audrey, 70

Statues, 19–20, 91, 95, 143

Straight-line theatres: Agora, 36–37; Attica, 35–36; Dionysos, 36–39; eighth-century Greek sites, 30; Lato, 30–31; Lenaion, 37; Magna Graecia, 33–34; Minoan/ Mycenean, 28; North Africa and the Islands, 35; Pelopennesos and Boeotia, 31–33

Stratou, Dora, 25

Sturzbecker, Russell L., 22 n. 1

Suda, 1, 12, 45–46, 56

Taplin, Oliver, 1, 68, 70, 81, 121, 136, 162

Theatres: Agora (Athens), 36–37, 99; Aigina, xiv, 105, 106; Aizanoi, 143;

Akrai, xv; Alabanda, 144; Alinda, 142, 144; Amnisos, 30; Antiphellos, 144; Aphrodisias, 77, 144; Apollo Erethemia, xiv, 105; Apollonia, 105; Aptera, xiv, 105; Argos, 11, 17, 26, 27, 31, 33, 36, 40, 47, 48, 99, 142, 143; Arykanda, 144; Aspendos, 106, 144; Assos, 144; Balbura, xiv, 144; Balbus, 142; Buthrotum, 105; Butrinto, 47, 53, 57; Byllis, 105; Catania (Katane), 35, 105, 106; Chaironeia, 27, 31, 33, 100, 142; Corinth, 11, 27, 31, 47, 51, 53–55, 61 n. 31; Cyrene, 35; Delfi, 17, 144; Delos, xv, 21, 44, 105, 107, 141; Dion, xv, 106, 142; Dionysos (Athens), 11, 24, 27, 38–39, 43, 47–48, 56–57, 59, 109, 110, 116 n. 19, 124, 141, 149; Drero, 30; Efesos, 144; Epidauros, xiii, 24, 26, 40, 43, 44, 47, 48, 70, 95 n. 9, 97, 116–117 n. 24, 141, 143, 144; Eretria, xv, 11, 24, 47, 48, 106, 110, 142, 144, 149; Fiesole, 144; Gournia, 28; Gytheion, 144; Halikarnassos, 47, 55; Heraclea al Latmos, 144; Herculaneum, 17, 142; Herodes Atticus, 143; Hierapolis, 97, 100, 143, 144; Iasos, 144; Ikaria, 27, 35, 39; Isthmia, 31, 47, 48, 57, 77; Kabirion, 47, 55, 105; Kalasarna, xv; Kassope, 101; Kaunos, 143–144; Kephalos, 47, 51–52, 57; Kibyra, 144; Knossos, 25, 28; Kyanae, 144; Laodicea, 144; Lato, xv, 30, 47, 50, 57, 106; Lenaion, 27, 37; Letoon, 144; Locri, 33, 106; Lymira, 144; Magnesia, 144; Mallia, 28; Mantinea, xv, 105, 142; Marcellus, 142; Messene, 105; Metapontum, xv, 106, 142; Miletus, 144; Minturnae, 144; Morgantina, 33, 40, 47, 50, 57, 59; Munychia, 35; Mycenae, 39, 41 n. 28; Myra, 143–144; Nea Pleuron, 105; Nysa, 144; Oenanda, xiv-xv, 144; Oeniadae, 144, 146 n. 9; Orange, 144; Orchomenos in Arkadia, xv, 47, 51, 57, 59; Orchomenos in Boeotia, 39; Oropos (Amphiarion), 27, 31, 35, 77, 116–117 n. 24, 144–145; Ostia, 142, 144; Patara, 144; Pergamum, xv, 17, 44, 144; Pergamum (Asklepion), 47, 55–56; Perge, 143, 144; Phaistos, 28; Philippi, 47,

48, 57; Pinara, 144; Piraeus, 43, 144; Poliochni, 28; Pompeii, 17; Pompey, 142, 144; Priene, 24, 44, 47, 50, 57, 60 nn. 23 & 24, 77, 89, 122, 144; Prusias ad Hypium, 144; Rhamnous, 27, 35, 39; Rhodiapolis, 144; Rome, 146 n. 7; Sagalassos, 144; Sagunto, 140, 144; Samothraki, xiv; Sardis, xiv, 105; Segesta, 11; Segobriga, 144; Selge, 144; Side, 106, 143, 144; Sikyon, 11, 24, 88, 142; Stratonikea, 144; Stratos, xiv, 105; Taormina, 144; Tegea, xv, 31, 105–106, 142; Telmessos, 144; Termessos, 144; Thera (Santorini), xv, 35; Thorikos, 17, 18 n. 30, 27, 33, 35, 36, 39, 40, 44, 47, 49, 57, 60 n. 21, 87, 144; Timgad, 143; Tlos, 143; Trachones, xv, 35, 36; Vergina, 39, 47, 48, 60 n. 18; Verulamium, 143, 144; Zaragoza (Caesaraugusta), 140, 143

Theoris, 45

Thespis, 21, 45, 63

Third actor, 128–133, 136, 165, 168–172, 175–176, 179

Threshing circle, 24, 25–26, 44

Thymele, 42–48

Thyroma stage lighting, 95, 116 n. 21

Timocrates, 81

Touring, 68, 110–113

Tragedies, 2, 3–5, 6, 7, 9, 42, 44, 62, 64, 65–66, 70, 75, 78, 81, 85, 88, 89, 118, 120, 121, 122, 123, 125, 128, 129, 130, 136, 165, 166–167, 173, 174, 176; happy endings, 6, 166–167; play schedule, 112–113, 123

Trendall, A. D., 46, 72, 88, 91

Trireme, 114

True, Marion, 159

Vergil, 159

Vignola, Giacomo Barozzio, 92–93

Vince, Ronald, 1

Vitae, The, 12, 14 n. 28

Vitruvius, 10–12, 25, 26, 46, 70, 71, 78, 80 n. 20, 84, 92, 95, 107, 141, 142, 144, 145

Webster, T. B. L., 46, 70, 72, 88, 90, 91, 147, 152

Winkler, John J., 64, 130

Winter's Tale, 179

Wirsing, Heinrich, 146 n. 9

Wooden theatres, 17, 18, 26, 36–37, 39, 47, 66, 68, 71, 76, 108, 120, 136

"Wright" and "write," 137 n. 3

Würzburg *skene* fragment, 66, 73, 75, 87, 130

Xenophon, 26, 68

Zuntz, G., 4

STUDIES IN THEATRE HISTORY AND CULTURE

Classical Greek Theatre: New Views of an Old Subject
  By *Clifford Ashby*

Marginal Sights: Staging the Chinese in America
  By *James S. Moy*

Melodramatic Formations: American Theatre and Society, 1820–1870
  By *Bruce A. McConachie*

Meyerhold: A Revolution in Theatre
  By *Edward Braun*

Modern Hamlets and Their Soliloquies
  By *Mary Z. Maher*

Our Moonlight Revels: *A Midsummer Night's Dream* in the Theatre
  By *Gary Jay Williams*

The Performance of Power: Theatrical Discourse and Politics
  Edited by *Sue-Ellen Case* and *Janelle Reinelt*

The Recurrence of Fate: Theatre and Memory in Twentieth-Century Russia
  By *Spencer Golub*

The Show and the Gaze of Theatre: A European Perspective
  By *Erika Fischer-Lichte*

Textual and Theatrical Shakespeare: Questions of Evidence
  Edited by *Edward Pechter*

The Trick of Singularity: *Twelfth Night* and the Performance Editions
  By *Laurie E. Osborne*

Wandering Stars: Russian Emigré Theatre, 1905–1940
  Edited by *Laurence Senelick*